Editor-in-Chief and Founder:
  Lyndon H. LaRouche, Jr.
Editorial Board: *Lyndon H. LaRouche, Jr. , Helga Zepp-LaRouche, Robert Ingraham, Tony Papert, Gerald Rose, Dennis Small, Jeffrey Steinberg, William Wertz*
Co-Editors: *Robert Ingraham, Tony Papert*
Managing Editor: *Nancy Spannaus*
Technology: *Marsha Freeman*
Books: *Katherine Notley*
Ebooks: *Richard Burden*
Graphics: *Alan Yue*
Photos: *Stuart Lewis*
Circulation Manager: *Stanley Ezrol*

INTELLIGENCE DIRECTORS
Counterintelligence: *Jeffrey Steinberg, Michele Steinberg*
Economics: *John Hoefle, Marcia Merry Baker, Paul Gallagher*
History: *Anton Chaitkin*
Ibero-America: *Dennis Small*
Russia and Eastern Europe: *Rachel Douglas*
United States: *Debra Freeman*

INTERNATIONAL BUREAUS
Bogotá: *Miriam Redondo*
Berlin: *Rainer Apel*
Copenhagen: *Tom Gillesberg*
Houston: *Harley Schlanger*
Lima: *Sara Madueño*
Melbourne: *Robert Barwick*
Mexico City: *Gerardo Castilleja Chávez*
New Delhi: *Ramtanu Maitra*
Paris: *Christine Bierre*
Stockholm: *Ulf Sandmark*
United Nations, N.Y.C.: *Leni Rubinstein*
Washington, D.C.: *William Jones*
Wiesbaden: *Göran Haglund*

ON THE WEB
e-mail: eirns@larouchepub.com
www.larouchepub.com
www.executiveintelligencereview.com
www.larouchepub.com/eiw
Webmaster: *John Sigerson*
Assistant Webmaster: *George Hollis*
Editor, Arabic-language edition: *Hussein Askary*

EIR (ISSN 0273-6314) *is published weekly (50 issues), by EIR News Service, Inc., P.O. Box 17390, Washington, D.C. 20041-0390. (703) 297-8434*

European Headquarters: E.I.R. GmbH, Postfach Bahnstrasse 9a, D-65205, Wiesbaden, Germany Tel: 49-611-73650
Homepage: http://www.eir.de
e-mail: info@eir.de
Director: Georg Neudecker

Montreal, Canada: 514-461-1557
eir@eircanada.ca

Denmark: EIR - Danmark, Sankt Knuds Vej 11, basement left, DK-1903 Frederiksberg, Denmark. Tel.: +45 35 43 60 40, Fax: +45 35 43 87 57. e-mail: eirdk@hotmail.com.

Mexico City: EIR, Sor Juana Inés de la Cruz 242-2 Col. Agricultura C.P. 11360 Delegación M. Hidalgo, México D.F. Tel. (5525) 5318-2301
eirmexico@gmail.com

Copyright: ©2017 EIR News Service. All rights reserved. Reproduction in whole or in part without permission strictly prohibited.

Canada Post Publication Sales Agreement #40683579

Postmaster: Send all address changes to *EIR*, P.O. Box 17390, Washington, D.C. 20041-0390.

Signed articles in *EIR* represent the views of the authors, and not necessarily those of the Editorial Board.

What Really Happened in China?

What Just Really Happened in China? You Have to Find Out for Yourself!

Nov. 16—Helga Zepp-LaRouche, the founder of the Schiller Institutes, today called on the American people to disregard the press blackout and the lies by the U.S. and European media about President Trump's China trip—and instead to find out for themselves the truth about the historic development that took place there. Speaking on her regularly scheduled weekly webcast Zepp-LaRouche said:

"I think it's very important that our U.S. viewers and businesses around the world really take a look at this yourself; do not go by what the media are reporting. Try to get the speeches, which are all archived; listen to them yourself. Go to Chinese television. This is really an appeal to people's reason, not to be fooled by the media, and not to fall into the trap of Cold War propaganda. What is happening is just the opposite of what the media is saying. Please, our listeners and viewers—meaning you—take the time to inform yourself; develop your own judgement. You don't have to believe us—but try to go to the original sources and get a first-hand opinion of what is really happening, instead of relying on the media."

In her webcast, Zepp-LaRouche gave her viewers a short summary of what actually took place on that trip:

"I think it is the beginning of a new era of strategic relationships between the United States and China, as Chinese President Xi Jinping has said. Their characterization of what they did in welcoming Trump and giving him the highest possible honors, was that this was a 'state visit-plus.' President Xi even called it a 'state visit-plus-plus.' They rolled out the red carpet, so to speak, in a way that they have never done for any other foreign dignitary since before the founding of the People's Republic of China.

"What they did, was they had a first day of introducing President Trump to the ancient culture of China. For that purpose, they closed down the Forbidden City for an entire day, and then they had a gala dinner in one of the palaces. They showed him three different Beijing operas, and they showed him the restoration of ancient art and crafts, and similar things. But of course, President Xi Jinping was the tour guide for all of this. Anybody who has ever read or listened to his speeches, knows that he is very well cultured in Chinese history, but also in universal history; so this was really an incredible tour. And there were other aspects of the visit, such as trade deals for $253 billion. And when President Trump came back from the Asia trip, he said that he had deals for about $300 billion, but that that was only be the beginning, and soon it would be tripled.

"But I think what was much more important, as much as the economic deals are important—I don't want to neglect that—but I think much more deeply important was the deep human accord between these two Presidents. I'm going to do something which I normally don't do, but given the fact that the media has distorted what happened in this visit so much—if they reported it at all—I want to read to you a passage from what President Trump said in commenting on this reception. He said:

Yesterday, we visited the Forbidden City, which stands as a proud symbol of China's rich culture and majestic spirit. Your nation is a testament to thousands of years of vibrant, living history, and today it was a tremendous honor to be greeted by the Chinese delegation right here at the Great Hall of the People. This moment in history presents both our nations with an incredible opportunity to advance peace and prosperity alongside other nations all around the world. In the words of a Chinese proverb, 'we must carry forward the cause, and forge ahead into the future.' I'm confident that we can realize this wonderful vision, a vision that will be so good and in fact so great for both China and the United States.

"And then he continued:

So we come from different places and faraway lands. There is much that binds the East and West. Both our countries were built by people of great courage, strong culture, and the desire to trek across the unknown into great danger that they overcame. The people of the United States have a very deep respect for the heritage of your country and the noble traditions of its people. Your ancient values bring past and future together into the present. So beautiful! It is my hope that the proud spirits of the American and Chinese people will inspire our efforts to achieve a more just, secure, and peaceful world. A future worthy of the sacrifices of our ancestors and the dreams of our children."

Zepp-LaRouche singled out as an example, the disparaging coverage in the German "newspaper of record" the *Frankfurter Allgemeine Zeitung*, which called the Chinese treatment of President Trump, "pomp" and a "Chinese deception game."

"The true picture is not the picture of Trump you get from the media. As a matter of fact, I have never seen such an outrage and such cynicism as what is now being expressed against Trump, with the exception of what has been said against my husband. And similar treatment is being given to President Putin and President Xi. But anybody who has ever been in the Forbidden City, which was the palace of the Chinese Emperor since the 15th Century—you cannot but be impressed by the majestic architecture, the beauty of the construction, the furniture, and the whole display of Chinese art. To call that mere 'pomp,' just shows you how absolutely ignorant these scribblers really are."

Zepp-LaRouche said that the promise of good relations between China and the U.S.A. being brought about by Presidents Trump and Xi, is now urgently needed. The common interest of mankind urgently requires that the U.S.A. reawaken its industries and rebuild and enhance its infrastructure. This can be accomplished if the U.S.A. joins China's Belt and Road Initiative. Last Spring, Zepp-LaRouche had said that if President Trump joined the Belt and Road Initiative and repaired U.S. relations with China and Russia, "He could be one of the greatest U.S. Presidents of all time." After the Beijing trip, she added, "Trump is actually doing it."

"So, I'm confident that the opportunity is there for a new renaissance, for an uplifting of people in which the best traditions of all cultures—of all nations and cultures of this planet are revived; and out of that, the new renaissance can be created. I think that that is an absolutely realistic possibility. So, be happy and join us!"

"Now we need each of you to join a national mobilization, so that everyone can find out how historic this visit of President Trump to China actually was, what the potentials are for the American people, and why President Trump's assailants must not succeed. Join us—the fate of the U.S.A., and actually the whole world, depends on it. Be an American, so that there can be 'America First.' And that is not in contradiction to what president Xi calls 'A community of shared future for mankind.'"

EIR Contents

www.larouchepub.com Volume 44, Number 47, November 24, 2017

White House

Cover This Week

President Trump participated in the APEC Summit, Nov. 11, 2017.

WHAT REALLY HAPPENED IN CHINA?

Trump's Asia Trip: Thinking Comes First

by Dennis Speed

Nov. 21—Seeking to counter the poisonous effects of pragmatism upon his Chinese countrymen, Dr. Sun Yat-Sen—the great revolutionary who so deeply admired Abraham Lincoln and his Trans-Continental Railway system, that he reproduced that concept and design in his own 1921 book, *The Industrialization of China*—insisted: "Doing is easy; thinking is hard." In that vein, if Americans wish to figure out what to do to extricate ourselves from the greatest crisis to face this country since the death of Franklin Roosevelt in 1945, they should listen to these wise words. "Doing is easy; thinking is hard."

A dialogue was convened in Manhattan on Sunday, Nov. 12, immediately after the showing of the film, *A Good American,* a documentary about National Security Agency (NSA) whistleblower and master code-breaker, William Binney. That the symposium, moderated by journalist Sean Stone, also included several opponents of the Russiagate hoax, including Binney himself, was important in its own right. Beyond exposing that hoax, the panelists struggled to answer the question of why, apart from the well-documented corruption, Constitutional violations, and malfeasance by the NSA and other intelligence agencies, Russiagate was actually occurring—other than "to impeach the President." Helga Zepp-LaRouche, upon being briefed on the meeting, observed that what must be supplied for the participants in such discussions, is an explanation of why the Russiagate attack against the President is being pursued in the first place.

In a statement now circulating in the United States,

EIRNS/Michelle Fuchs

(Above) Panel in New York City after viewing the movie, "A Good American," about William Binney. (Right) Video grabs from the movie, showing Binney and Diane Roark.

both in the streets and through social media, entitled "Americans Must Discover What Really Happened on Trump's China Trip," Zepp-LaRouche makes the following appeal: "I appeal to your reason not to be fooled by the media, not to fall into the trap of Cold War propaganda. The opposite of what the media is saying is happening. Please, dear listeners and viewers—meaning you—take the time to inform yourself; build your own judgement." An accurate evaluation of President Trump's recently concluded trip, and its actual accomplishments, including his "informal discussions" with Vladimir Putin, requires deep thinking, free of "Big Brother's" snap judgements and suggestions that are too readily supplied by the "Wikipedia social media pop culture."

President Trump's visit to China dwarfs that of Nixon's 1972 trip in its potential importance to the United States, to China, and to the world. It is of a completely different nature, in no small measure affected by the role of Lyndon LaRouche and Helga Zepp-LaRouche in China during the past 25 years. China's 1972 condition, and that of the United States, when compared to 2017, are now, while not reversed, certainly opposite in impulse-tendency. Optimism characterizes China's 1.4 billion population, while a "no future" outlook dominates the people of the United States. President Trump seeks to change that, but the opposition to his doing so is being manifest in many quarters. Russiagate is its most noxious, as well as its most vulnerable expression.

Crisis of the Presidency

When, in mid-October, President Trump insisted that CIA Director Mike Pompeo meet with William Binney in order to find out "what really happened with Russiagate," everyone familiar with Binney's notorious battle with the NSA, going back to the September 11, 2001 attacks on the World Trade Center, recognized the implications of this implicit endorsement by the President of Binney's competence. Prior to that, on Sept. 9, *Executive Intelligence Review* had hosted a New York City meeting at which Binney had appeared and had discussed the Russiagate matter thoroughly.

A few days before that Manhattan meeting, Binney was covered on CBS News, CNN, *RT* (formerly *Russia*

Stephen F. Cohen, professor emeritus of Russian Studies at New York University and Princeton University, noted President Trump's effort to avoid a new cold war with Russia.

Today), and in various printed media, which only later, after Nov. 7—beginning with Glenn Greenwald's publication *The Intercept*—reported the Pompeo-Binney meeting, which itself had actually taken place on Oct. 24. Veteran Intelligence Professionals for Sanity (VIPS) founder and former CIA analyst Ray McGovern—part of a panel that included former House Intelligence Committee staffer Diane Roark and William Binney—told the 350 people assembled Nov. 12 at Symphony Space, "never in my life did I expect that the President of the United States would call the head of the CIA and say, 'Hey, I got this memo from Veteran Intelligence Professionals for Sanity, and I want you to go talk to the guy who wrote it, Bill Binney.'"

Trump's single-minded and almost single-handed crusade to avoid a new Cold War with Russia, despite opposition in his own administration, was noted by Stephen F. Cohen, professor emeritus of Russian Studies at New York University and Princeton University, in a piece entitled, "Russiagate Zealots (Mainly Democrats) Have Become a Major Threat to U.S. National Security," published in *The Nation* magazine, Nov. 15.

This was a "watershed" piece for Cohen, considered by most to be a prototypical "New York liberal," inclusively in his role as a contributing editor of *The Nation*.

Cohen has contended that the present "crisis of the American Presidency" is far worse than that which occurred around Nixon and Watergate: "unlike Trump, President Nixon was never accused of 'collusion with

the Kremlin' or faced reckless, and pre-
posterous, allegations that the Kremlin
had abetted his election by an 'attack on
American democracy.' "

Mark of the British Beast

While this is formally true, it does
not take into account the deployment of
"public diplomacy," that is, "grey" and
"black" propaganda, by sectors of the
intelligence community, against the
President of the United States. Trump's
intention to clean out the intelligence
agencies, announced in the first days of
his Presidency, has not endeared him to
those Obama-era holdovers who are
adept at deploying the more refined
"psychological warfare" interagency
capabilities that were established by the
Reagan-era National Security Decision
Directive 77, authored by Walter Ray-

Reagan Presidential Library

LaRouche opponent Walter Raymond smiles. The CIA's Walter Raymond, Jr., sits between President Reagan and his National Security Adviser, John Poindexter.

mond. Also, Cohen is perhaps unfamiliar with the historical role of the Congress for Cultural Freedom's
(CCF's) cultivation of what is sometimes called "right-
wing social democracy," actually neoliberalism, and
its (in fact, though not in form) nearly identical twin,
neoconservatism. While the CCF is typically and mistakenly identified as a CIA-based "arts and literature"
operation of the Soviet Union era, the roots of the CCF,
as with the roots of Russiagate, are British. The British
Information Research Department, a successor organi-
zation to its war-time Political Warfare Executive
(PWE), founded in 1948, was the true controlling
agency of the Congress. This "special relationship" did
not end in 1967, with the "exposure and shutdown" of
the CCF. The Christopher Steele dossier in the Russiagate case, as with the "Downing Street Memo" in the
lead-up to the 2003 Iraq War, is the paw-print which—
unlike the traces of Cyrillic that were left by the myth-
ical "Guccifer 2.0 hack"—actually identifies the "mark
of the British Beast."

Donald Trump's "so much for the special relationship" remarks addressed to visiting British Prime Minister Theresa May in March, less than two months after
his inauguration, and his insistence that he "would not
be lectured to" on climate change and other British im-
perialist schemes by the daffy Prince Charles, have
produced the most pronounced rift with Britain since
the Eisenhower and Kennedy eras. Trump has yet to

visit London. His personal relationships with Xi Jinping, and with Vladimir Putin, are—as with the relationship established between Lyndon LaRouche and
Ronald Reagan from their encounter in New Hamp-
shire in 1980—of paramount importance. Therein is
contained the promise of the future of humanity in our
time. The President of the United States, when prepared and inclined to do so, can overcome the control
and power of British intelligence over American foreign policy and domestic policy, and assert not merely
national self-interest, but the General Welfare of humanity as a whole. The Preamble of the Constitution of
the United States, in its General Welfare clause, gives
him or her not only the right, but the sworn responsibility to do so.

To this point, Cohen was right to observe,

What Trump did in Vietnam last week was therefore vitally important and courageous, though
uniformly misrepresented by the American
mainstream media. Despite unrelenting "Russiagate" attempts led by Democrats to impeach
him for "collusion with the Kremlin" (still without any meaningful evidence), and perhaps even
opposition by high-level members of his own
administration, Trump met several times, infor-
mally and briefly, with Russian President Vladimir Putin. Presumably dissuaded or prevented

by some of his own top advisers from having a formal, lengthy meeting, Trump was nonetheless prepared. He and Putin issued a joint statement urging cooperation in Syria, where the prospects of a U.S.-Russian war had been mounting. And both leaders later said they had serious talks about cooperating on the crises in North Korea and Ukraine.

What the President said in Vietnam about the relationship between that nation and the United States was of particular note as well. He defined a commonality of outlook between the United States and Vietnam

White House video

U.S. President Trump and Vietnam President Quang at joint press conference in Hanoi, Nov. 11, 2017.

as best expressed in the two countries' fierce commitment to independence:

> In America, like every nation that has won and defended its sovereignty, we understand that we have nothing so precious as our birthright, our treasured independence, and our freedom.... As an old man, just before his death, [Founding Father John Adams] was asked to offer his thoughts on the 50th anniversary of glorious American freedom. He replied with the words: "Independence Forever."
>
> It's a sentiment that burns in the heart of every patriot and every nation. Our hosts here in Vietnam have known this sentiment not just for 200 years, but for nearly 2,000 years. [Applause] ... Today, the patriots and heroes—[applause]—of our histories hold the answers to the great questions of our future and our time. They remind us of who we are and what we are called to do.

In acknowledging Vietnam's 2,000-year struggle for sovereignty, in the same breath as his invocation of the American Revolution, Trump showed the people of that nation a willingness to reconcile the horrific mistakes of the past in favor of a new harmony of interests—including harmony between Vietnam and its 2,000-year adversary, China.

One of America's Finest Moments

The actions taken by President Donald Trump since mid-October, his "on the plane" discussions with the press on Putin's insistence that there was no Russia hack, and his insistently repeated idea that a relationship with Russia was "a good thing, not a bad thing," may be one of the few things preserving this nation's security and preventing the outbreak of global war, including thermonuclear war. Trump's intuition was correct, that his own institutional intelligence capabilities, including the CIA and NSA, were hopelessly politically compromised and unreliable, and must be immediately corrected and upgraded. That view prompted the President's personal intervention to employ competent patriotic "mavericks," such as William Binney, who in turn has deployed other members of the Veteran Intelligence Professionals for Sanity (VIPS). These individuals, putting aside partisanship, are once again serving their country, not as adversaries to it, but as fierce opponents of those who would betray it, and its President, for the greater glory of the British empire.

The decision to do this—to both keep Trump's Presidency alive, and to keep his breakthrough policy of alliance with China and Russia moving forward, even in the face of the terror campaign being carried out by Special Executioner Robert Mueller—will be seen in the future, despite all present indications to the contrary, as one of America's finest moments.

The War on (British) Drugs Has Begun

by Paul Glumaz

Nov, 21—Though it is very little reported, especially in the mainstream media, the first year of the Trump Administration has seen the emergence of the beginning of a war against the decades-long British-directed efforts to corrupt the nation and destroy the wills and minds of the U.S. population through drug trafficking and drug addiction. This is not the least of the reasons for the heavy British involvement in the Russia-gate coup against Trump, and the antics of former FBI director, and now Special Counsel, Robert Mueller.

Donald Trump has begun to fight the opioid epidemic, Britain's and Obama's final solution for America.

President Trump, joined by the First Lady, signs a Presidential Memorandum on Oct. 26, 2017, ordering the Acting Secretary of Health and Human Services to declare the opioid crisis a national public health emergency.

On Oct. 26, President Trump addressed the existential crisis of opioid addiction and drug abuse in America. First and foremost, in this address Trump declared a public health emergency, in which he directed all agencies to use the emergency authority that the President was granting to them, to deal with the crisis. The President also announced that the National Institutes of Health (NIH) and private partners will embark on a crash program to develop non-addictive pain-killers to begin replacing opioid use. Included in Trump's address was the initiation of a campaign against the culture of drugs, an awareness campaign on the dangers of opioids, and a massive increase of federal funds to local facilities to treat drug addiction, including treatment in the prison system. A further step was to empower and encourage multiple jurisdictional efforts to indict and try pill-mill doctors, and to launch civil lawsuits at the state level and below, against pharmaceutical companies for deceptive advertising and promotion of pharmaceutical opioids among the medical community.

But Trump's address was not just about opioid addiction. It was also about shutting down the gangs that are at the center of the distribution of illegal drugs, as well as shutting down the importation of drugs, and working with other nations, "whether China, or any other country," to shut down the cartels and the international production of drugs.

Notwithstanding a general media black-out, the war on drugs has begun.

On Nov. 7, twenty-eight Wisconsin counties began suing drug manufacturers to recover their costs of battling the opioid crisis. The lawsuits claim that county services have been overwhelmed by the effects of the epidemic, and the manufacturers must reimburse the local governments. The companies being sued are:

- Perdue Pharma,
- Teva Pharmaceuticals,
- Johnson and Johnson,
- Cephalon, and
- Endo Pharmaceuticals.

This is the beginning of a nationwide movement of lawsuits by local and state governments against Big Pharma. Quincy will shortly become the first city in Massachusetts to sue the pharmaceutical industry for downplaying the dangers of opioids. Similar suits are being prepared in Chicago, Seattle, and Ohio.

On Nov. 14, Indianapolis, ravaged by the opioid epidemic, began a similar suit alleging deceptive marketing practices. But it is in West Virginia, the state worst affected by the opioid crisis, that billions of dollars are being sought in reimbursements.

A similar situation is emerging in New Mexico, where eight opioid manufacturers are being sued.

Doctors are being arrested all around the country, and some are being charged with second degree murder.

To properly understand the immense importance of this initiation of a war on drugs by Donald Trump, one must understand what happened under the Obama presidency. The key is that the creation of the drug epidemic was intentional, and Obama was part of that intention. The intent was to destroy the soul of our nation. A nation that succumbs to drug addiction, drug trafficking, drug legalization, and the culture of drugs with its corruption and its criminality, is a defeated nation, just as if an invading army had subjugated and occupied it—perhaps worse.

Now that a war on drugs has begun, there is hope that a growing popular resistance movement against the drug-trade will develop. One of the problems, however, is that the major media is blacking out the actions of the Trump Administration to dampen any tendency for such a resistance to emerge.

Six Components of Britain's Drug War

1. The pharmaceutical component. The pharmaceutical companies' misleading opioid promotion program has brought addicting opioids to the doctor's office, and then into every home and into every community in the nation. This transformation of much of U.S. medical practice into an addiction machine is perhaps the single most destructive process overseen by the Obama Administration. Once addiction has occurred via the doctor's office, the way is open for the expansion of street heroin as a cheaper substitute for the prescription opioid. Prior to the increased role of pharmaceutical companies in promoting addiction, drug addiction began in the streets—now it starts in the doctor's office.

The agency which polices the pharmaceutical dispensing of opioids is the Drug Enforcement Administration (DEA). Under Obama, DEA enforcement of the laws on opioid prescriptions was very lax, almost nonexistent, at the same time that pharmaceutical companies geared up extensive, misleading campaigns to persuade doctors to prescribe opioids for every kind of pain, including the usual kickbacks for the doctors who

Logos of the five pharmaceutical companies being sued to recover the costs of battling the opioid crisis.

do so. This culminated in the passage by Congress of the "Ensuring Patient Access and Effective Drug Enforcement Act of 2016." The final version that was unanimously passed by Congress was negotiated by Senator Orrin Hatch with Obama's DEA.

On Oct. 15, 2017, the *Washington Post* published an article that described how major pharmaceutical companies spent $102 million to lobby Congress from 2014 through 2016 to get the bill passed. The pharmaceutical companies' all-too-willing partner in this was the Obama Administration and Obama's DEA.

The purpose of the Ensuring Patient Access and Effective Drug Enforcement Act of 2016, was to weaken aggressive DEA enforcement efforts against drug distribution companies that were supplying corrupt doctors and pharmacists who peddled narcotics to the black market. The law basically gave the pharmaceutical companies self-policing powers. It essentially codified, and made much worse, the already lax enforcement situation, by making it virtually impossible for the DEA to

FBI arresting suspected members of the MS-13 gang in New York City.

U.S. Secretary of State Rex Tillerson (R) and then Secretary of Homeland Security John Kelly (L), at a press conference in Mexico City, Feb. 23, 2017.

freeze suspicious narcotic shipments from the companies. According to the DEA's chief administrative law judge, quoted in that article, ending the DEA's power to freeze suspicious shipments removed the ability of the DEA to prevent masses of pharmaceutical opioids from reaching the street.

On top of the already-existing problems of illegal drug trafficking, bringing the pharmaceutical companies in to assist in dramatically expanding drug addiction can be considered in terms of its effects on the citizens of this nation, to be the "final solution."

2. The street gang component. The British empire has always euphemistically called criminal gangs "mediating structures," that is, ruling structures that are outside the law. They have always been a crucial part of the British empire, both past and present. The spectacular growth of such "mediating structures" in the U.S.A. in the last decade is staggering.

According to the FBI, there are currently 33,000 violent street gangs, motorcycle gangs, and prison gangs with a total of 1.4 million members which are criminally active in the U.S.A., including Puerto Rico. Perhaps not all of them distribute narcotics. However, the street gang, as a "mediating structure," can become the local franchised sales force for the larger drug cartels, while being economically maintained and supported by them.

One of the biggest and most violent of these gangs is the Mara Salvatrucha gang, or MS-13. According to *Time* magazine, it has 6,000 members in the United States. Other sources say it has up to 10,000 in the United States, and 70,000 in total for all North and Central America. MS-13 plays a significant role in partnering with various Mexican drug cartels in the distribution of narcotics in the United States. In the period of April to May of this year, the Justice department, at the instigation of Donald Trump, rounded up 1,400 gang members, many of them key leaders of MS-13. Nothing like this had been done before on such a scale. This act by the Trump Administration indicates a potential for much greater roundups in the future.

3. The drug cartel component. The Mexican Sinaloa cartel is thought to control a majority of the U.S. drug market. Another five or so Mexican drug cartels control most of the rest. The drugs could be coming from anywhere in the world, although most probably come from south of the U.S. border. The cartels act as the wholesaler and work with the street gangs as the retailers. It is estimated that the drug traffic accounts for $64 billion in sales in the United States, and $50 billion in Mexico.

There are many scandals, such as "Fast and Furious" and others, that indicate not just tolerance of the Obama Administration for the Mexican drug cartels, but that these two were mutually supporting. Obama's presidential campaigns were supported financially by the cartels, and the cartels were supported with weapons to increase their violent subjugation of the Mexican people.

General John Kelly, now Trump's Chief of Staff, as

EIRNS/Dean Andromidas

Dr. Antonio Maria Costa, former director of the UN Office of Drugs and Crime, showed drug trade liquidity was laundered by the deregulated banks.

cc/www.stephan-roehl.de

George Soros, a big funder of drug legalization, is a leading political activist for the London-centered financial system.

well as Trump himself, have alluded to the need to fully involve the United States in helping the Mexican authorities wage a war against the Mexican drug cartels.

4. The financial component. A huge flow of cash from the drug trade ultimately finds its way into the international banking system. One such bank that was caught laundering drug money in the many billions of dollars was HSBC. There are many others. In an extensive interview, Dr. Antonio Maria Costa, the former director of the UN Office of Drugs and Crime (UNODC), showed that the growth of money-laundering proceeds historically from the growth of financial deregulation and the expansion of the offshore tax havens. The growth of financial speculation and derivatives creates a great incentive for the liquidity of the drug trade to leverage speculation. According to Italian author Roberto Saviano, "London is the world center of drug money laundering."

Restoring Glass-Steagall protections will help law-enforcement shoot down drug-money laundering. A serious war on drugs will have to deal with this financial aspect.

5. The liberal and legalization component. The campaign for legalizing marijuana, whose most prominent figure is George Soros, connects the financial component to the propaganda and political-action component. George Soros is the leading political activist for the London-centered financial system. Whether Soros is funding overthrowing governments in the billions of dollars, funding Obama, or funding drug legalization, his

"Open Society" network is the exemplar of a liberal and permissive attitude to drug consumption and drug addiction. The idea that it should be permissible for an irreplaceable human being—with all the efforts and all the hopes society has placed in that human being—to be destroyed by drug addiction, is criminal. Nothing will demoralize and corrupt a society more than such a conception. President Donald Trump cannot wage a successful war on drugs without ultimately dealing with this. One can expect a future mobilization on this from the Trump Administration. This was implied in his Oct. 26 address.

6. The promotion of a "cop killing" culture. Obama is culturally considered the "the rapper in chief." The rap culture has a strong anti-law enforcement aspect. Cops are considered racist killers, and drug gangs are the persecuted racial victims of white oppression. Much of the rap culture promotes, along with a violent attitude toward law enforcement, the rape of women. It is a culture of rage and violence. It is the cultural face that justifies gang rape and gang intimidation of entire communities. To have a President such as Obama, so prominently associated with rap culture and with the culture of gang rape, is coherent with the British intent of subjugating the United States through drug addiction and a drug culture. Donald Trump has repeatedly indicated an intolerance for this gang culture, and has stated a commitment to end the reign of terror that it currently exerts in communities all over the nation. This is also a key part of the war on drugs—a war which everyone should support.

President Trump's Asia Trip Steps Into the New Paradigm

This is an edited transcription of Helga Zepp-LaRouche's Nov. 16 weekly webcast for the Schiller Institute or La-Rouchepac.com.

Harley Schlanger: Hello, I'm Harley Schlanger from the Schiller Institute, and I'd like to welcome you to this week's webcast with Helga Zepp-LaRouche, the founder of the Schiller Institutes.

Obviously, the main topic for this week is going to be the recently-concluded trip of President Trump to China. This was quite spectacular, and as we've been reporting, it represents a decisive shift away from the old policy, the Obama policy of the Asia pivot, into a potential era of cooperation and peaceful development. It was clear from the first summit that took place in Mar-a-Lago, that Trump and Xi Jinping—the President of China—have a very good relationship. It seemed to be developed further on this trip.

So, what are the results in your view, Helga, of this trip? And what are the broader strategic implications of what's going on, given the successful completion of this trip?

Helga Zepp-LaRouche's answer to host Schlanger's first question, is incorporated into the editorial statement above, which leads this issue of EIR.

Schlanger: And I think we probably should point out a little bit more of this media coverage, just to cite

U.S. President Donald Trump and his wife Melania Trump (L), and their hosts, China President Xi Jinping and his wife Peng Liyuan, in front of Taihedian, the Hall of Supreme Harmony, during their visit to the Palace Museum (in the Forbidden City), Beijing, Nov. 8, 2017.

two examples. The *Washington Post* has an op-ed saying that Trump's trip was not the total fiasco most people expected. And an unidentified *Financial Times* correspondent is quoted, "I have to think that in some ways, the Asian leaders are laughing behind his back, and certainly the Chinese are." Now, at the same time, in the United States, as you pointed out, there is an attack on Xinhua, the Chinese press service, saying that they probably should register as foreign agents. And *Russia Today* is now already being put under that form of sanction: They have to register as foreign agents.

We've discussed this before, Helga, but the question keeps coming up. Why is the media doing this? What is it that they're so fearful about in the prospect of cooperation between the United States, Russia, and China? I want you to just review that again.

Zepp-LaRouche: An article appeared just today by Willy Wimmer, who was State Secretary of the German Defense Ministry (like a U.S. Undersecretary of Defense) in 1988-92 under Helmut Kohl. He wrote that the media are absolutely like Goebbels. That is true, if one considers that the British, at the end of the Second World War, studied the methods of Goebbels, and they concluded that you have to out-Goebbels Goebbels. They did a pretty good job of that by perfecting the method of total propaganda—as Bertrand Russell said—we have to make sure that the people believe that snow is black and that black is white. Once we have accomplished that, then we have done our job. That's exactly what they are doing.

People who are subjected to this kind of permanent bombardment with propaganda, cannot possibly even imagine that governments actually exist which are devoted to the common good of their people. But I have made the point repeatedly that anybody who studies it, has to come to the conclusion that a country which lifts 700 million people up out of poverty, and has a clear strategy to get everybody out of poverty by 2020, is devoted to the common good of the people. There is really nothing debatable about it. When China offers the world the Belt and Road Initiative, China is offering that kind of economic development model—the Chinese economic miracle—to other countries, which obviously understand that this is much more attractive than being a submarine in the Pacific for NATO or for some other militaristic group.

The oligarchy, that is, the people who have been conducting geopolitics at least since the emergence of the British Empire, designed the post-World War II order after Truman took power in the United States under Churchill's influence. While there were certain changes and interruptions with de Gaulle and with Kennedy and with other leaders, there has been a continuity from that period. What you see right now in the United States is on the one hand a full-fledged McCarthyism:

Sidney Hook, speaking on June 26, 1950 at the opening session of the founding of the Congress for Cultural Freedom in West Berlin.

They never noticed that the Soviet Union has disappeared, that Communism is no longer there, but instead you now have Russia which is not communist. But they have kept the same methods of the Cold War, in order to influence the opinions of the people against Russia and China. They were the ones who tried to create a unipolar world after the Soviet Union disintegrated in 1991, using policies of color revolutions and regime-change, which were all based on lies.

All of these things happened, but I want to move to another subject, which is the exhibition which is taking place in Berlin right now, portraying the history of the Congress for Cultural Freedom (CCF).

This is an institution financed by the CIA from 1950 to 1967, which waged cultural warfare. I did some studies about it some years ago, and it is the most unbelievable operation. At the height of this cultural warfare, this operation owned 120 magazines, and they organized all the musical concerts. They replaced Classical music with modern music; they promoted so-called "expressionist" modern art. They had professors on their payroll, as well as students, journalists, and trade unionists. They just penetrated every possible institution in order to promote their model of so-called "freedom," because people were attracted by the Soviet Union in the postwar period, and this CCF operation was used to put an end to that. Most of these left-wing intellectuals didn't notice who was behind it, but if they did notice, they were sworn to secrecy with the threat of 20 years in jail if they revealed it. This is something people should really study, because this is not something which stopped in 1967, but it continues to operate to the present day.

There was a very revealing article in the *Frankfurter Allgemeine Zeitung*, which said that what is so upsetting about this exhibition, is that it reveals that this CCF operation of the CIA was not done to promote some reactionary outlook, but that it brought to the fore exactly that left-liberal paradigm which is now the politically correct view held by the entire Western establishment. It is that paradigm which is now being challenged by Russia, by China, by Islam, and by the populist parties of the West.

I find this quite an admission, to say that the present paradigm of political correctness is the result of a CIA operation. People have to really think about that, because that is really is what is behind the ferocity of the attacks against Trump. That is why, for example, I would guess, Nancy Pelosi is so absolutely anti-China, which is noted even by the Chinese now, who say that the entire success of Trump's Asia visit is being attacked just for the sake of U.S. domestic political fights. It is ridiculous to take a strategic relationship of such importance between the two most important countries in the world, and make an internal political squabble of it.

Harley, you have to say something on the CCF as well, because I think it's important for our viewers that this really sinks in, because this is why people often have such ridiculous views, and they aren't even aware of it.

Schlanger: I think this is very important, and it's something that you've repeatedly talked about over the years. One of the main intentions we had in making this webcast was not just to bring out the truth against the filth of the fake news which is 24 hours a day, 7 days a week—but to raise this more profound question of the nature of man. The aim of the Congress for Cultural Freedom is precisely to spread the idea that man is driven by animal instincts. Therefore economy must be organized around greed and self-interest, and people should be focused on their own immediate enjoyment and pleasure. This goes back to Bentham and Adam Smith and the British empirical school. The fact that this was imposed by the CIA—and there are many, many documents that verify this, as you mentioned, from the magazines, the reports, and the journalists. There was a German editor not that long ago, who said that all German news was filtered through the CIA, that in a sense, the journalists were all on the payroll. So, it does continue.

Now this is something that the Schiller Institute was uniquely set up to combat. Not just the idea that when you tell the truth, that will lead people into a new paradigm; but that people need to reflect on what is the actual nature of man. Are we just animals—are we just beasts and creatures of comfort?

It's also worth noting that this same grouping, which is now attacking Trump, President Xi, President Putin, and others, was the group that targetted your husband, Lyndon LaRouche, and put him in prison in 1989, through the work of George Herbert Walker Bush and others. He was deemed a threat to this system. And the person who oversaw that case against LaRouche, was none other than the amoral legal assassin himself, Robert Mueller. I think it is important—and people can go to the Schiller Institute, or go to larouchepac.com, and there's plenty of material on the Congress for Cultural Freedom. This is quite significant.

Helga, my question for you is: These are also the same people who created the European Union, and are now promoting this idea of destroying national sovereignty. I wonder if you'd like to just add to that?

Zepp-LaRouche: The whole idea of a united Europe, the idea of a Europe of the regions, going back to the Pan-European Union, to Coudenhove-Kalergi—these were the same people who believed in "racial hygiene." They admired Hitler's race laws. This grouping helped to bring Hitler into power. The form this takes now, is that because of the absolutely unjust economic policies of the Troika [European Commission, European Central Bank, and the International Monetary System] imposed on Europe, there is now a dissolution of Europe. The East European countries are turning away, and the separatism in Spain is now spreading. There is actually the possibility that the EU is not going to last in its present form.

There was a rather remarkable study by the Bundeswehr (German army) in February, which predicted six different scenarios under which the EU would cease to exist, leading to, in the worst case, in which most of the European member states joining a Russian bloc by 2040.

The EU in its present form as a supranational institution, has taken away more and more of the sovereignty of its member nation-states, and cannot survive. That is why we are also warning that we really have to pay attention to the fact that the next financial crash is about to happen. The EU has just once again eliminated the possibility for the separation of commercial banks from investment banks, as happened with Franklin Roosevelt's Glass-Steagall act. They have once again permitted the use of the same kind of derivatives which made the 2008 crisis so devastating.

So, I think we need a new conception. We have said many times that we have to move to a completely new basis for international relations, where sovereignty is respected, and where differing social systems are respected. We need to have a new paradigm where mankind comes first, where the common aims of mankind are put before all differentiations into national interests. That is exactly what Europe has to orient to if it is going to survive.

Schlanger: I think if people listen clearly to the quote you read from President Trump in China, you see that kind of spirit reflected in what he said. It was a very interesting speech. Also, what he said in Vietnam, where he talked to the people of Vietnam about how we share the horrible effects of the Vietnam War, and that when we honor veterans, we honor them not for fighting, but for reflecting a commitment to a principle of the nation. I think we're beginning to see this reflected in what the President is doing.

In this context, we now have all the new stories coming out trying to defend the Steele dossier, and the *Guardian* of London is taking the lead in this; it has taken the lead in this from the beginning. But for instance, in his discussion with the press after his brief meetings with President Putin, President Trump unloaded on Clapper and Comey and Brennan and others. Where do you think the Russia-gate attack stands right now, with all the investigations and information that has come out?

Zepp-LaRouche: If you listen to the media, at least

Senator Grassley's office

Senator Chuck Grassley, Iowa, Chairman of the U.S. Senate Judiciary Committee.

in Europe, you would never find out about it, because you would only hear new allegations about the supposed collusion of Trump's son and what-not. But the fortunate development is that there are several initiatives coming from the Congress and from the Senate, which put the spotlight exactly on the FBI, on the collusion with British Intelligence, and on the question of what was the role of Hillary Clinton. Why did the Obama Administration co-finance the "dodgy dossier" of Christopher Steele? This comes from several Congressmen who have written an open letter asking Attorney General Sessions to appoint a special investigator to investigate all of that. Then in the Senate, Senator Grassley is continuing to put the spotlight on these questions, so I think it's a battle. It's not yet decided. I think there was a new barrage against Trump when he came back, and there are several Congressmen who started an impeachment procedure against Trump, which I don't think has any chance of success at all. But it is just more mud being thrown, and judging from what President Trump said on the plane when he flew to Vietnam, he really was very clear which side committed the crimes. I can only hope that his spirit, which was reinforced on his trip to Asia, will carry through, and there will be an investigation of all of these people. I think it's much more hopeful than you would assume if you only listened to the media—because I think that there is a certain determination coming from many sides. It's coming from the Tea Party, and it's coming from the Bernie Sanders' supporters.

And there was just a very important event on Sunday, Nov. 12 in Manhattan, where William Binney, Diane Roark, Ray McGovern, and Sean Stone, showed the movie "A Good American," which portrays the work of William Binney, who was in the fourth most important job in the NSA, when he resigned in protest after September 11th happened. He said that what was implemented then, went completely against the ethics of a patriotic intelligence person in the United States. Therefore, he left the NSA. And now he has proven with forensic evidence that there was no Russian hacking. President Trump asked CIA Director Pompeo to meet with Binney to review this evidence—which did not prevent Pompeo from repeating the statement afterwards that there was Russian hacking. But I don't think this line will hold up.

What is at stake is that the crimes of that apparatus could be exposed big-time, and I think that would really liberate the entire world, if this operation could finally be terminated.

Schlanger: One final point on that, was the interesting parallels between recent statements by President Trump and people like President Putin and Russian Foreign Minister Sergey Lavrov—that they've identified these problems as coming not from the current Trump Administration, but from Obama. There's a mythology that continues in the media that Obama solved the economic crisis, and that he was actually much better at international relations. I don't know if you remember this, Helga, but on his last trip to China, in contrast to the greeting given to President Trump—when President Obama got off the plane for the G-20 summit, they had no stairway to let him get down from the plane. He was stuck for twenty minutes on Air Force One. So this idea of Obama as being the great hero, is one of the things that is going to have to be challenged.

Just finally, on your sense that we now have moved into this new Europe. What do you expect in the weeks ahead with the Chinese initiatives and what will come out of Europe and the United States in reaction to these initiatives?

Zepp-LaRouche: I think Europe is in a very shattered condition. Maybe a "Jamaica" coalition can be formed in Germany; (It's called the Jamaica coalition because the colors of the parties making it up are those of the flag of Jamaica.) But they have not come up with answers to any important questions. They are discuss-ing the most unimportant issues, and I think this is not going to be of any lasting significance. [*Editor's note: coalition talks broke down on Nov. 19.*]

The other European countries are in disarray. At the same time, there is a groundswell of industrialists and other groupings wanting to join the Silk Road. Right now in Germany, in Hamburg, in Bremen, in Frankfurt, in Dusseldorf, in Stuttgart, and in Munich, business groupings and chambers of commerce are organizing conferences or friendship societies. So, there is a groundswell of people recognizing that there is a new paradigm developing, and they want to be part of it. Given that, in Eastern Europe, Central Europe, the Balkans, Italy, Spain, Portugal, Switzerland, Austria, and France, very important voices are calling for this.

For example, French President Macron sent Raffarin, the former prime minister, to attend the Beijing Belt and Road Forum in May. He gave a very good speech. Now, another former French prime minister, Dominique de Villepin, also came out and praised the 19th Congress of the Communist Party of China, saying that this was absolutely in line with the aspirations of Europe for peace, for cooperation, and for a multi-polar world. So, what I'm saying is that while the EU in Brussels, and unfortunately Berlin, are putting on the brakes in respect to joining this new paradigm, there is a groundswell of more and more people who realize that that is really the way to go.

I would think that the impact Trump's Asia trip has a similar effect in the United States. Especially those states which are immediately affected by his economic and trade deals, such as West Virginia, Ohio, Alaska, and a couple of others—I think all together a total of twelve states have been affected positively by economic deals.

I think the word will spread, and one of the purposes of this webcast is to bring people up to date, to point your attention to these developments, and to actually ask you to help. This webcast is meant to get people active. Join the Schiller Institute. Help us to spread the conception that a new relationship among nations is absolutely possible, and it's already becoming a reality. Don't sit on the sidelines. Become active with us, because this period has a tremendous potential.

Last week we talked about the fall of the Wall and the great historical chance that that represented. But I think if you look at the possibility that mankind can move to a completely new era where there is prosperity for everybody and peace among nations, this defines a

Dominique de Villepin in 2010.

cc/Marie-Lan Nguyen

new era of civilization. I have the complete conviction that—provided that there is not some great tragedy like a financial crash for which no solution is implemented in time, or some other crisis kicked off around some incident, some fake story—I think that the new world view is taking over.

The popular culture of the West has become a culture where everything is allowed, where there are no criteria, there is no standard, no morality—that is something which will not last. It is a false belief, it's an ideology, a deviation from the true nature of man, and I think it will disappear in a similar way to the way scholasticism disappeared, because it was an inadequate idea associated with a certain period of history in Europe originating in the Middle Ages. And it vanished. Today, you don't have scholastics, at least not in this old form.

So, I'm confident that the chance is here to have a new renaissance, to have an uplifting of people, where the best traditions of all cultures, of all nations and cultures of this planet are revived, and out of that development, a new renaissance can be created. I think that that is an absolutely realistic possibility. So, be happy and join us!

Schlanger: Well Helga, thank you for your optimism and your work in spreading the spirit of the New Silk Road. We'll see you next week.

Rediscovering the Mind
Of Lyndon LaRouche

by Robert Ingraham

Nov. 20—In January 2017, prompted by Helga Zepp-LaRouche, *Executive Intelligence Review* initiated a project to begin republishing major works by Lyndon LaRouche. During the past eleven months we have run forty-six of these articles. As we approach the one-year anniversary of this project, it is time to reflect on the importance of this undertaking, particularly in light of the great new possibilities which have arisen on the world stage since the inauguration of Donald Trump as President of the United States, also in January this year.

As of November 2017, human society is poised for perhaps the greatest transformation in the entirety of its existence. This current opportunity is best described as being a "Shelley Moment." This is a time, as Percy Shelley writes in his "A Defence of Poetry," when "there is an accumulation of the power of communicating and receiving intense and impassioned conceptions respecting man and nature. The persons in whom this power resides may often, as far as regards many portions of their nature, have little apparent correspondence with that spirit of good of which they are the ministers."

Witness the recent—and mis-reported—visit to China by President Trump Nov. 8. Place that Presidential visit in the expanding global reality of the "win-win" Belt and Road Initiative. We are at the potential starting point of a new era for humanity, one governed by the Westphalian Principle of the "Benefit of the Other," and one characterized by unprecedented progress in science, economic development, and human progress. This is a moment at which history can change, and this is precisely the breakthrough for which Lyndon LaRouche has been fighting for more than sixty years.

LaRouche's personal courage and the works produced by his mind have created the potentials which now exist. Despite persecution, imprisonment, and ostracism, he has persevered. His is the greatest mind of our time. If we are to turn the current possibilities of

Lyndon LaRouche, interjecting the topic of strategy to deal with the threat of World War III, in a Jan. 22, 2014 discussion of the properties of Moon soil with Natalie Lovegren of the LaRouche PAC Science Research Team. The broadcast was moderated by Creighton Jones (right).

this moment into a victory, it is vital that growing numbers of individuals take up the study of LaRouche's works—to engage his mind at the highest possible level.

A Real Cultural War

Before turning to the subject of LaRouche's writings, one essential—if dirty—piece of business must be dealt with. This difficulty defines both the obstacle and the opportunity for success.

Nations and peoples throughout the world are now jumping on the Belt and Road express. They want a future. The optimism radiating out of China is now spreading throughout the world. The obstacle to this becoming a universal paradigm lies within the trans-Atlantic culture of Europe and the United States. Much of the population in the trans-Atlantic world seems incapable of grasping the great opportunity which now presents itself. The very idea of a beautiful positive future has become alien to them.

Beginning after the death of Franklin Roosevelt, and escalating dramatically following the murder of John F. Kennedy, the trans-Atlantic world has undergone a deep cultural collapse, one which is still ongoing. This did not just "happen." The spread of cultural pessimism and anti-human values was created by the oligarchical families of Europe, their aristocratic friends in the United States, and the British Monarchy. The origins of our current malaise go back even further, to the post-1815 "Romantic movement" and the devastation of World War I. By the 1920s, oligarchical-sponsored groups such as the Frankfurt School—and its many offshoots and derivatives— were already engaged in all out war to eradicate the Renaissance tradition in western culture, to deny the existence of human reason, to abolish the Promethean identity of Man, and to spread pessimism throughout the population.

This oligarchical project took a giant leap forward with the 1950 creation of the Congress for Cultural Freedom (CCF), leading to a direct attack on the classical Renaissance tradition in both art and music. Under the direction of the CCF, irrationality, Dionysian Eros, and literal psychosis were championed as great art and music. The last great classical conductor, Wilhelm Furtwängler, was persecuted, while the Nazi Herbert von Karajan was promoted. Great paintings were removed from museums and replaced by fecal smears on a canvas or "primitive art."

Then came the 1960s, with the San Francisco Diggers' admonition to "do your own thing" and "if it feels good do it." A culture was created based on reducing the individual human identity to its most bestial content—a culture dominated by Eros, with higher human cognition discouraged and removed. As a result, today, many people are afraid of science, terrified of human progress, pessimistic about the future, and certain that mankind is destroying Mother Earth. We have reached a point where many 16-30 year-olds can't even figure out what sex they are, and where drug addiction is simply considered a "lifestyle choice."

There are many today who proclaim that what is needed is a "cultural war" to rid America of its growing resemblance to Sodom and Gomorrah. Those efforts will fail without the guidance of Lyndon LaRouche. It is not enough to simply be "against" moral corruption. Nor is just preaching religious doctrine going to work. What is at issue is the nature of Man. A "Christian" who believes in environmentalism is already on the road to degeneracy. What LaRouche asserts is the paramount importance of the magnificent heritage of Western culture. From Plato, through to Dante, Nicholas of Cusa, Gottfried Leibniz, and others, the core of western culture and progress has been located precisely in that quality which absolutely separates human beings from all other animals, i.e., Man's ability to reason, to create through a lawful process of hypothesis, to discover new hypotheses. It is precisely the re-awakening of that power of the human mind which is urgently required today in Europe and America, and it is precisely within the Shelley Moment defined by the Belt and Road initiative that such a restatement of the human identity becomes possible

We should settle for nothing less. In this fight would it not make sense to utilize the greatest weapon in our arsenal? Should not the Mind of Lyndon LaRouche be brought into this battle?

Project LaRouche

During the past year, four reading groups have been created to study and discuss some of LaRouche's articles, including those recently republished in *EIR*. Two of the groups are in Virginia, one in New Jersey, and one in northern California. Among the articles read and discussed have been: "Leibniz from Riemann's Standpoint," "On LaRouche's Discovery," "The Substance of Morality," "How to Tell the Future," "On the Subject of Education," "Mathematics & Measurement," "The Science of Physical Economy," "The Truth About Temporal Eternity," and "On the Subject of Metaphor." All may be found on the *EIR* website.

This article will not attempt to reproduce the content of any of the aforementioned articles, nor to delve too deeply into the discussion process surrounding those readings. What will be stated here is that what has defined these study groups is a commitment by the participants to not merely quote from Lyndon La-

LaRouche talking to young people after his July 20, 2006 webcast.

Rouche or to talk *about* his ideas, but to grapple with the mind of the man himself. At the heart of many of the discussions has been the proposition that "the issue is not what you think but *how* you think," i.e., that real knowledge does not arise from accruing "information," but in the rigorous realm of verifiable human hypothesis.

This question of the human cognitive identity and true social evolution arose in many different ways during the readings. Points of discussion have included LaRouche's notion of Anti-Entropy; his concept of Higher Hypothesis, which has given mankind a method of provable validity; and his discussion of the relationship of the One to the Many, i.e., the universal to the particular, which is relevant to both biology and mankind's relationship with the universe.

A featured topic in many of LaRouche's writings lies in his concept of physical economy, an economic approach which, again, flows from the human creative identity. A great deal of discussion has taken place on the subject of "free energy," and the necessity for that free energy to increase even while the "energy of the system" is also increasing. This then led into an examination of the question of the Productive Power of Labor. Needless to say, a mastery of this concept, and its implications, is of urgent importance given the opportunities presented by the Belt and Road today.

In at least three of the reading groups, extended discussion took place on the subject of LaRouche's insights into Gottfried Leibniz' *Monadology*, particularly as to the nature of the Monad and the relationship of the Monad to Creator. In at least one instance, this led into an extended discussion of Leibniz versus Newton on the Calculus. In New Jersey this also provoked a consideration of John Sigerson's work on *Motivführung* and the question of classical composition.

Not all of the questions raised in LaRouche's writings were "solved." In one group an extended discussion took place on the subject of isentropic compression and its relation to economic forecasting, without fully resolving all of the issues involved. The readings and the discussions involved hard work.

Making People Human

One might imagine a *musikabend* at the home of the Mendelssohns or a poetry reading with Shelley, Keats, and their friends—events where human creativity becomes the subject of discussion. Perhaps the LaRouche reading groups have not yet reached such lofty heights; yet one after another of the participants has described the experience as a "reawakening of a part of your mind that you haven't been using," of being able to "relate to people on the basis of ideas," and being "blown away."

One participant even stated that the change in people was visible, that he noticed a "brightness in people's eyes, more upright posture, mutual self-respect, and less anger." Another participant also mentioned a "respect for the dignity of each other's mind."

A key to the process has been a willingness of the participants—in the tradition of Cusa's *On Learned Ignorance*—to re-examine what one thinks one knows, to not be afraid to ask "What did LaRouche mean by that"? Yes, creativity is a product of the individual sovereign mind, but working through the challenges raised by Lyndon LaRouche—and then being willing to engage in a dialogue with others—has the effect of transforming the underlying relationships among the people involved. The New Jersey group has even adopted the name of "The Union of Ignorance," and what has been constant through all the groups is a quality of "humbleness" and a willingness to enquire and to discuss the ideas presented by LaRouche.

Creativity will dry up if it is not used. People give in to practicalities, day-to-day concerns, or the mind-deadening bureaucracy of their workplace. The next thing you know, they're carrying around grudges and repressed anger. That, of course, is where the true power of classical art, theater, and music comes into play. The problem today is that most people in the trans-Atlantic world have become so bestialized and pessimistic that they don't even open themselves up to great art. They won't "go there," because their self-enslavement is so powerful.

That is where Lyndon LaRouche comes in. LaRouche goes right to the heart of the issue: "Are you human, or are you a monkey?" If you are human, what does that mean? What is it that distinguishes you as human? What is it that made possible the upward progress of the human species? Relentless, LaRouche takes no prisoners; he simply provides hope to all. As one participant in the reading groups stated, "LaRouche's Mind is at the center of being able to make world history."

This latter point gets to the most important aspect involved in the study of LaRouche's writings, for what he is discussing is the quality of mind whereby an individual may affect the future. These are not academic exercises, but a social process whereby greater cognitive powers might be brought into the battle for the future of society.

The Battle Defined

We live within a trans-Atlantic culture where not only is every form of human degradation paraded on television and the internet, but where the very substance of human thought is under attack.

During the late 1940s and early 1950s, Lyndon LaRouche undertook an in-depth critique and refutation of the proposals of John von Neumann (*Theory of Games and Economic Behavior*—1944) and Norbert Wiener (*Cybernetics: Or Control and Communication in the Animal and the Machine*—1948). Central to LaRouche's rebuttal was his insistence that human thought, i.e., the method of Platonic hypothesis, could not be reduced to a mechanical or mathematical model. Fast forward 70 years. Today, von Neumann's and Wiener's progeny, the icons of Silicon Valley and the information age, are hegemonic as to the nature of human cognition. The leaders of Facebook, Wikipedia, Twitter, Craigslist, Microsoft, and Apple have now been at it for forty years of creating a society based on linear digitalized information. Human creativity has been reduced to the "clever" ability to write sophisticated binary "computer algorithms," capable of predicting and manipulating the behavior of a people who themselves have been reduced to sub-human linear thought. These are also the techniques which today dominate the financial institutions of London and Wall Street.

Sadly, in Europe and America this Eros-driven information age is now omni-present. Most people under the age of fifty have no concept of what a human culture—a human identity—actually is. Nevertheless, there are three powerful sources for hope in this situation:

First and foremost is the leadership now flowing from China, particularly in the global implications of the Belt and Road. The involvement of Russia along with many other nations, and now joined—minimally at least in intent and friendship—by Donald Trump, holds great promise for the future. Stupendous promise.

The second cause for optimism is to be found in the human spirit itself. Despite two to three generations of degradation, every human individual still possesses within himself or herself the power of agapic creativity, and the reality is that many, many young people today—despite their confusion and mis-education—are yearning for something better. Many know that there is more to life than drugs and video games. They need to be engaged.

Finally, we have the mind of Lyndon LaRouche. What LaRouche does is challenge people. He demolishes the comfortable axioms that are "common sense" to the majority, and he provokes their minds to work. Forcefully. Many others look for "agreement," for practical compromise. LaRouche holds high the banner of Prometheus, and he offers a choice: Do you want to be human—or would you rather be a monkey?

EIR is republishing the works of Lyndon LaRouche for a reason. We urge you to take up the challenge.

What Economics Must Measure

by Lyndon H. LaRouche, Jr.

By the time this edition of *EIR* appears in the mailboxes, yet another, world-wide round of market disasters will have wracked the tortured, and doomed international financial and monetary system. The persistence of the October-November series of "crashes," which continue to ricochet throughout world financial markets, have begun a very worrisome, 1997 Christmas season. For the remaining, relatively short time ahead, we acknowledge the conjecturable possibility, that desperate monetary authorities might resort to a hyper-inflationary explosion, modelled upon the torment of 1922-1923 Weimar Germany. Otherwise, contrary to U.S. Federal Reserve Chairman Alan Greenspan's wishful delusion, this barrel has no bottom.

For sane people, world wide, the only reason for hope is, that the President of the United States, together with other relevant heads of state, will act to create a new world monetary system, soon. To avoid an otherwise inevitable plunge into global chaos, we must have a "New Bretton Woods" arrangement, replacing the hopelessly doomed present "IMF system," with a new system which is modelled on successful features of the pre-1959 monetary and related practices.

One may hope that U.S. President "Bill" Clinton's successful, Washington, D.C. meeting, with China's President Jiang Zemin, signals an outbreak of much greater pungency and force, in confronting the United States' London-steered political enemies, both within the U.S.A., and abroad, than we had seen from the "White House" quarter since Franklin Roosevelt and John Kennedy. If we are wishfully overestimating the Clinton White House, there is no cause for celebrating "our present way of life," by the time Christmas—or, the November U.S. Congressional elections—comes due in 1998.

The Great Council of Venice: woodcut from a 1578 edition of Gasparo Contarini's Della Repubblica (inset: the Venetian Lion of St. Mark). The world's current crisis, LaRouche writes, presents us with the opportunity to free mankind of the succubus of the Venice-style financier oligarchy, which has preyed upon the economies of nations for 500 years.

For thinking people, the most important questions are, "Why was this crisis inevitable? Why is the only hope, a 'new Bretton Woods' agreement, ending former U.S. President George Bush's foolish flirtation with a globalized 'new world order,' for a return to the United States' patriotic economic tradition?" The only alternative to despair, lies in returning, at long last, to those "anti-globalist," protectionist economic policies which shaped all past periods of net improvement in the prosperity of the United States and all of its people.

Today, months after the Thailand crisis of early July, only persons who are ignorant, or who are blinded by wishful superstition, could still doubt, that the collapse of this present financial system is inevitable. Today, in hindsight, the statistics showing ratios of financial obligations to real assets, are in focus. The practical question is: "To whom could we turn, to inform us what must be done, to rescue the nations and their populations from the inevitable doom of this financial system?"

The key follow-up questions are:

"Why did those in charge wait so long to see this coming? Why did our governments not change their policies in time to prevent this? Should we entrust the making of policy now, to the judgment of persons who imposed and maintained this failed system during the past thirty-odd years, especially the lunatic policies of the more recent eight years?" It is time to remember, that these failed policies were the work of persons who dominated, increasingly, the positions of power and influence in the U.S.A. during the recent thirty-odd years to date, people who clung so stubbornly, so long, to the terrible, ideological errors which this doomed system represents.

"What is the error in thinking, of nearly all leading economists, and many others, which caused them to reject" my own, often-rejected, but now irrefutable forecast of the present breakdown-crisis of the global system?

The latter is no obscure consideration. Among notable economists, I have the best record in long-range forecasting, during the recent forty years.[1] Yet, despite all the supporting evidence which had been accumulating over recent decades, especially since the events of August 1971, until the small beginnings of a change, during 1993-1994, my warnings were rejected, at least in effect, by all but a few leading economists of North America and Europe, and many elsewhere, too. Recent months' events have now supplied much wider circles a shocking demonstration of the intellectual bankruptcy of those in economic policy-shaping who rejected those forecasts. Until that terrible blunder in my opponents' thinking is identified, and corrected, what person would trust the judgment of such experts, and still pass for a rational person, today?

In addressing that not-uninteresting question, it should be evident, that the principal source of my political opponents' failure, is not some isolated error of oversight; the source of their recurring blunders has been, specifically, that faulty kind of so-called "mainstream, post-industrial utopian thinking," which has dominated both private and public policy-shaping institutions, increasingly, during the recent decades. Under the circumstances of a global crisis, which most of them said, until most recently, could not happen: "What are the relevant, characteristic flaws presently embedded in both today's educational systems and so-called 'mainstream thinking'?"

For the answer to the latter question, we must look to the recent decades' trends in thinking among the professors and textbooks at relevant institutions of higher learning. We must focus upon that faulty, "politically correct" ideology, which dominates the institutions which have misshaped the popular ideology among, especially, the "under 55" generations of the United States and western Europe today.

Now, since the fact of the global financial collapse is

---

1. For example: (a) During 1959-1961, I forecast that, under a continuation of the kinds of axiomatic assumptions which had dominated economic policy-shaping during the Truman and Eisenhower administrations, the existing international monetary system would undergo a succession of shocks during the second half of the 1960s, leading into a breakdown of the existing Bretton Woods agreements, and, that if those axioms were continued beyond that breakdown, the result would be changes parallelling those "Schachtian" austerity measures introduced into post-1931 Germany under Brüning and Adolf Hitler. (b) Speaking as a candidate for the Democratic Party's 1980 U.S. Presidential nomination, during mid-October through early December 1979, I repeatedly forecast that the measures of "controlled disintegration of the economy," introduced by Federal Reserve Chairman Paul A. Volcker during mid-October, would lead into a steep recessionary collapse of the U.S. economy, with a plunge into that recession no later than February 1980. (c) Beginning February 1983, I repeatedly forecast, that if President Ronald Reagan were to offer the Soviet Union a certain type of cooperation, in development of new ballistic missile defense, and should the Soviet government reject that cooperation, the Soviet economy would collapse beginning approximately 1988. (d) During Spring 1987, into July 1987, I forecast a collapse of the New York stock-market during early to middle October. See "The Coming Disintegration of Financial Markets," *EIR*, June 24, 1994. Also published as a pamphlet by *New Federalist*, under the title "LaRouche's Ninth Forecast."

generally acknowledged, the crux of the matter, for economists and related policy-shapers, is a problem of economic policy which I have addressed in several recently published locations, including my November 5 address to a symposium on international monetary reform, held in Bad Godesberg, Germany.[2] On the latter occasion, I emphasized the danger in the now-increasingly popular blunder, of assuming that the tactics for dealing with the presently ongoing international financial crisis, might be found by treating the present crisis as comparable to that of 1929-1931.

Indeed, it is characteristic of the miseducation supplied in virtually all economics classrooms, that the professional's usual knee-jerk reaction to the mere thought of a possible, oncoming major financial crisis, is, still today, to look back to the developments of 1929-1931, as if that experience would serve as a model, for explaining and measuring the significance, and severity, of any apparent shock to a part or the whole of the world's financial system. Contrary to such views, the assumption that today's crisis is a cyclical crisis of the same species as that of the late 1920s and early 1930s, is an illusion with no scientific basis in fact; it is a very dangerous sort of illusion, if it is widely believed among policy-influencers at this time. The burden of that Bad Godesberg address, was to warn against that popular error of presumption.

"How do we take the 'jerk' out of 'knee-jerk'?"

To that purpose, it was necessary that I supply an accurate, if most unfavorable characterization of those modern abracadabrists, who rely upon currently-taught statistical methods of economic forecasting. At Bad Godesberg, I compared such persons, to those misguided astronomers, circa 1801, whose reliance on statistical methods of point-to-point analysis, was the cause of their failure to match Carl Gauss's successful forecast of the orbit of the asteroid Ceres. At Bad Godesberg, I emphasized, that we must now apply to economics, that superior scientific method, through which Gauss revolutionized astrophysics, geodesy, and electromagnetism.

I warned that we must not rely blindly upon mere mathematics. Although economics must deal with quantifiable magnitudes, the mere manipulation of such magnitudes, according to someone's statistical equation, could not, in and of itself, determine the trends toward the macroeconomic profit, or loss, of whole economies. We must look behind the mere statistical surface of things, to the social policies which underlie, and control, the significance of those activities we treat as the measurable inputs and outputs of the economic process.

I indicated there, that we must also follow Gauss's protégé, Bernhard Riemann. We must apply the methods developed by Gauss, as Riemann developed them further: *it is the curvature which must be adduced for small, even infinitesimal intervals of action, which reveals the specific, determining curvature of the same process considered as a whole.*[3] We must apply these methods, as Riemann did, to the comparison of differing manifolds.

I indicated, that from this standpoint in method, we must view the crisis reflected in 1929-1931 developments, as, relatively speaking, a cyclical crisis, as relatively analogous to the orbit of a planet or asteroid around our Sun; whereas, on the contrary, the internal characteristic (Gaussian curvature) of the 1987 stock-market "crash," and its continuation into the current, 1997 phase of the crisis, represents the present international financial and monetary system, not as a cyclical event, but, as on a terminal trajectory, which it could not, in any case, survive.

In my presentation to that symposium, I emphasized the underlying, related difference, in terms of social characteristics, between all modern business cycles,

---

2. Lyndon H. LaRouche, Jr., "1997 Is Not 1929: A Lesson From Carl Gauss," *EIR*, Nov. 21, 1997.

3. This issue, of the determining role, in the large, of non-linear curvature in the very small interval of action, was the concern which prompted Johannes Kepler to propose the development of a calculus to "future mathematicians," the calculus which Leibniz developed. Unfortunately, few presumably literate science graduates today have the slightest grasp of the significance of the fact that Isaac Newton never developed an actual calculus, and that the revised form of Leibniz's calculus introduced through Augustin Cauchy's sophistry, the "limit theorem," is no longer the Leibniz calculus which Kepler had specified. It was precisely the error of Leonhard Euler, on which Cauchy's revision is based, which Gauss understood, and successfully corrected, in his forecast of the orbit of Ceres. The entirety of the work of Gauss, Wilhelm Weber, and Bernhard Riemann, thereafter, is premised upon Kepler's and Leibniz's recognition that physical action is non-linear in the infinitesimally small, and that it is this non-linearity in the infinitesimal interval of real-life physical action which is key to understanding the principled determination of the same continuing process in its totality. We should not overlook the fact, that Cauchy's trick with fractions is often useful for those work-a-day forms of engineering work, in which calculations may be, and must be simplified. To carry that simplification over into the domain of serious scientific work, is incompetence rooted in scientific illiteracy. The most popular forms of present-day statistical analysis and forecasting are the worst cases of the catastrophes to which blind acceptance of Cauchy's revision may lead.

until the mid-1960s, and the new kind of systemic crisis which has been building up during the recent thirty-odd years. For most economists, and laymen, alike, the nature of this difference takes them into what is, for them, previously unknown territory. It is important, therefore, that I demystify those crucial, but unfamiliar connections and differences. We must clarify the connection between governing ideas of social practice, and the statistical-economic results which those ideas express on the surface of the economy.

Since approximately three-quarters of an hour had been allotted for my presentation, it was not feasible to do more there than to situate and to summarize those crucial issues. A transcript of that address has been published in the preceding edition of the weekly *Executive Intelligence Review*.[4] Here, I supply the required, expanded treatment of the same core-argument, respecting the social basis for mathematical economics. That is the subject, and purpose of this report.

Ideology versus Science

I report that emotive associations, much more than formal lapses of intellect, are the principal source of the difficulty which prevents today's typical professional, or layman, from recognizing the decisive role of social processes as such, in determining the effects which economic statistics measure. The strong emotional block, which reference to these issues usually awakens today, even among relatively better educated professionals, expresses two problems of modern European culture, pathologies which are centered in contemporary academic life.

The first of these two problems, is what Britain's C.P. Snow argued in his lectures republished as a book, a few decades ago, under the title of *Two Cultures*.[5] As matter of historical fact, the gradual takeover of Europe's culture, by the closely related methods of empiricism, Cartesianism, and philosophical Romanticism,[6] since the close of the Sixteenth Century, has created an arbitrary, false, but popular dichotomy between science and art. This is the phenomenon which Snow identified as "two cultures." That unnatural dichotomy of the human mind, has succeeded to such an extent, that, in some respects, intellectually and emotionally, the representatives of the two branches of studies—science on the one side; art, social studies, and statecraft, on the other—often behave almost as different species.

Therefore, the suggestion, that both science and art ought to be regarded as Kepler and Leibniz did, as subsumed by a common principle of Reason, tends to evoke impassioned, angered, and thoroughly irrational outbursts of sophistry, from among representatives of each of the two departments, especially during recent decades.[7]

Secondly, that "two cultures" problem, has been aggravated by the impact of the takeover of the minds of the post-World War II generations, throughout most of the planet, by a certain, axiomatically asocial, radically positivist form of existentialist outlook.

Notable on the latter account, is the relative hegemony, in today's philosophy departments, of such variously fascist or quasi-fascist philosophers as Friedrich Nietzsche, the American Anglophile school of irrationalism of pragmatists William James and John Dewey,[8]

---

4. Lyndon H. LaRouche, Jr., op. cit., *EIR*, Nov. 21, 1997.

5. C.P. Snow, *Two Cultures and the Scientific Revolution* (London and New York: Cambridge University Press, 1993 reprint).

6. The authoritative paradigm of Romanticism was derived from Immanuel Kant's attack upon Gottfried Leibniz, the central feature of Kant's celebrated three *Critiques*. This was formulated by G.W.F. Hegel's accomplice in the effort to destroy the influence of Leibniz and Schiller at Berlin University, Professor Karl F. Savigny. Savigny formalized Romanticism with his decree, that there is no knowable principle of Reason in art or law. He laid down the dictum, that there must be an hermetic separation between science (*Naturwissenschaft*) on the one side, and art and statecraft (*Geisteswissenschaft*) on the other.

7. During the present writer's life-time, the use of the word "practical" in connection with education had a very dirty meaning, becoming dirtier and dirtier as generations passed. Friedrich Schiller used the German term, *Brotgelehrte*, to describe this phenomenon as seen in his time. As I have stated in earlier locations, I translate Schiller's "*Brotgelehrte*" as, "people who learn to sing for their supper, not for the benefit of music." Most among those who entered university under the U.S. returning veterans' "GI Bill of Rights," were "playing catch-up," in a hurry to qualify for employment, and post-graduate economic family security, in a professional's career; and, institutions of higher education were more interested in providing the kind of assembly-line mass education which met the demands of that market, than burdening the student with the task of discovering whether or not what was learned was truthful. For most of these students, the passion of Socratic search for scientific truth in knowledge was put aside, out of lust for a "more practical" object, of learning to pass the kinds of examinations employed by production-line education. Nonetheless, those educational programs into which those returning veterans were absorbed, were an intellectual paradise, when compared with the intellectual bedlam of today's educational programs. Today, Orwellian "political correctness" has almost entirely supplanted the traditional forms of education ruled by Socratic passion for truthfulness. Here, we acknowledge the existence of this problem, but our emphasis is upon the axiomatic issues internal to the design of taught doctrines.

8. Just as we are instructed to overlook the fact that Prince Bernhard of the Netherlands was a member of Adolf Hitler's Nazi SS until the date of his marriage to the princess, so it is considered "politically correct" to

Nazi philosopher Martin Heidegger, German novelist Hermann Hesse, the "Frankfurt School's" Theodor Adorno and Hannah Arendt, Heidegger's clone Jean-Paul Sartre, Sartre's Frantz Fanon,[9] and such fascistic prophets of "digital virtual man" as Norbert Wiener and John von Neumann. Among those professionally qualified persons, who reached adulthood during the 1950s or earlier, the relevant facts of post-1964 changes in social policy, are more or less familiar; however, even among those matured strata, the functional connection of those facts to economic processes, is seldom understood in an adequate degree.

On this second point, it may be said, that the single most stubborn obstacle to rational thought about economics today, is an increasingly popular, existentialist, misconception of man and nature. The presently popular view of human nature, is a popularized, perverted view of the human individual, a perversion which is not merely consistent with the "virtual reality" cults of "information theory" and "systems analysis," but is often defended on the authority of those radical positivist's superstitions. In social practice, that perverted, "post-modernist" opinion has become deeply embedded, not only among the so-called "me" generation of 1968 fame, but also that generation's offspring, and victims, "Generation X." This perversion represents the individual person as fated to be more a feral creature, than a social one.

That perversion is typified by Nazi philosopher Heidegger's existentialist dogma, which portrays the individual as struggling to claw his, or her way to a moment of survival and pleasure in a jungle-like society, into which he, or she has been unwillingly "thrown" at birth. It is a notion of a society which is the adversary, an adversary which the feral existentialist individual, or "tribe" of the post-modernist type, must learn to cheat.

For the majority among these post-World War II generations, in both Europe and the Americas, the patriot's sense of the individual, as an efficient part of humanity as a whole, has been abandoned, or simply mislain. The typical individual of the current "now" generations, lacks a functional sense of history as a process. In place of earlier, civilized, moral conceptions of both history and society, the recent generations have adopted the utopian fantasy of a "globalist" planet, without nations.

The fantasies which govern these generations' behavior, are living nightmares, in which regressive groups of the highly suggestible victims of cultural shock, see themselves as members of post-modernist tribes, each living out a labile pursuit of momentary "relative truth." Under today's regimes of "political correctness," the putative "relative truth" of each "tribe" or individual, differs arbitrarily from the "relative truth" of the neighboring such tribes, and persons, each and all of whom deny the existence of any "external," common truth to which all mankind is equally subject.

The result of the mass cultural degeneration of this recent thirty-odd years, has been the increasing hegemony of an existentialist's notion of "cultural relativism." Among those so afflicted, there is a corresponding aversion to the fact, that the development of society is an expression of a process of converging and diverging long swings in scientifically validatable, or invalidatable *willful* changes of cultural paradigms. The influence of "cultural relativism" is correlated with a refusal, by these younger generations, during the recent thirty years, to acknowledge the fact, that, if a majority of any culture adopts assumptions of practice which are contrary to knowable, universal laws, that society is doomed, implicitly, scientifically predictably, by its own willful mis-choice of culture. We should recognize this principle, from reflection upon the process of degeneration which has gripped the recent thirty-odd years of European culture globally.

In consequence, among most persons typical of the generations under fifty-five years of age, today, there will be, initially, a more or less violent rejection of any discussion to the effect, that the present global crisis is chiefly the result of those post-modernist changes in culture, the which the "golden generation" of the 1968 university student has carried during its upward career-march through the leading public and private institutions.

Yet, despite that defiant resistance to truth, it is precisely that post-1963 cultural paradigm-shift, which is the source of the present process of financial, monetary, economic, and cultural collapse of our global civilization.

Similarly, typical representatives of the post-World War II generations, will tend to entertain the proposition, that some bad mistakes were made during the 1946-1966 interval: prior to the mass-outbreak of the "rock-drug-sex youth-counterculture," "post-industrial" utopianism, and post-1969 cults of neo-Malthusian "ecologism." However, even after the presently ongoing collapse of the financial system, a collapse which its generations' choice of cultural paradigm created, the same majority of those generations will, still, today, tend to reject any approach to even that topic, if it smells to them of what they might term "economic determinism."

If these generations persist, and succeed, in continuing to impose their "mainstream thinking" upon policy-shaping, then, be assured, not only is the present international monetary system doomed, but the entirety of global civilization with it. In that case, the entire planet will be plunged into chaos, in a manner echoing what was called Europe's "New Dark Age" of the mid-Fourteenth Century. Under those presently threatened conditions, the proverbial "Four Horsemen of the Apocalypse" would reign for two generations or more, until a significant portion of mankind has purged itself sufficiently of today's "mainstream thinking," to lead the world into some form of cultural and economic renaissance.

So, like Biblical Belshazzar's Babylon, all great empires have doomed themselves, leaving the hollowed ruins of their former glory to be pitied by whatever new cultures, sooner or later, emerged from the self-imposed doom of the old.

There, in this issue, lies the only true vital, strategic interest of the United States today. Any discussion of "strategic interest," which does not proceed from this vantage-point, is pathetically suicidal at best, and perhaps worse. The only available rational choice now, is between either those radical changes in policy which lead to the survival of civilization, or, to a New Dark Age which were inevitable, unless those cultural changes are made. Since that choice will determine the outcome of this presently concluding century, intelligent people will prefer to focus upon the subject-matter of this present report, rather than any different topic.

Consider, thus, the following summary of those issues of method, the which must be addressed as a pre-lude to any effort to define those new policies which meet the requirements of this point of strategic interest. Situate the discussion within the historical context of the issues.

The Modern National Economy

Readers of *EIR* are already familiar with the general case: The difference between higher apes and mankind, is located in those "mechanisms," by means of which mankind has escaped that range of several millions individuals, which has been the planet's estimable maximum potential population of apes, during the recent two millions years, to reach population-levels of perhaps two hundred millions human individuals by the Hellenistic period immediately preceding the Roman Empire, and to have risen, from a level of several hundreds millions, during the Fourteenth Century, to over five billions today.[10] (See **Figure 1.**)

This demographic progress, which sets the human species absolutely apart from, and above all other species, is the fruit of the innate cognitive potentials of the individual member of the human species. These cognitive powers are typified, among other ways, by the generation of subsequently validated new discoveries of physical principle.[11] The more such principles are accumulated by a society, the more rapid the realization and continued new discovery of such principles, as

____

10. See, for example, Lyndon H. LaRouche, Jr., "The Coming Pearl Harbor Effect," *EIR*, Sept. 12, 1997, pp. 29 and 31.

11. Note, those experimentally validatable new discoveries of physical principle which have the effect of being new axioms of a mathematical physics, are of the species known as "Platonic ideas," so distinguished from the inferior conceptions known as "sense-perceptions." The ideas which are implicitly presented as solutions for *metaphor* in Classical forms of art, are also of this same Platonic species of *ideas*. The Socratic dialectic method, underlying all of the dialogues of Plato, provides the rigorous basis for generating, for defining *ideas* in this sense. The passion of concentration, through which such *ideas* are generated (in science, as principles representing solutions for rigorously defined ontological paradoxes; in art, as *ideas* resolving Classical metaphors), is known in Plato's and the Christian Apostle Paul's writings as *agapē*, which is more or less loosely translated as the Latin *caritas*, or, still more loosely, as the King James Version's *charity*. This interdependency among Classical forms of creative Reason and *agapē*, is understood in Christianity (e.g., *I Corinthians* 13) as the *idea* represented by the notion of man and woman made in the image of God. This quality of thought and passion, is the notion of Reason in the work of Johannes Kepler, Gottfried Leibniz, et al., but neither *ideas* nor Reason exist in the work of those empiricists, Cartesians, materialists, positivists, Romantics, etc., whose intellectual ancestry is traceable to the Eleatics, Sophists, William of Ockham, Francis Bacon, Thomas Hobbes, Immanuel Kant, et al.

European population growth and life-expectancy

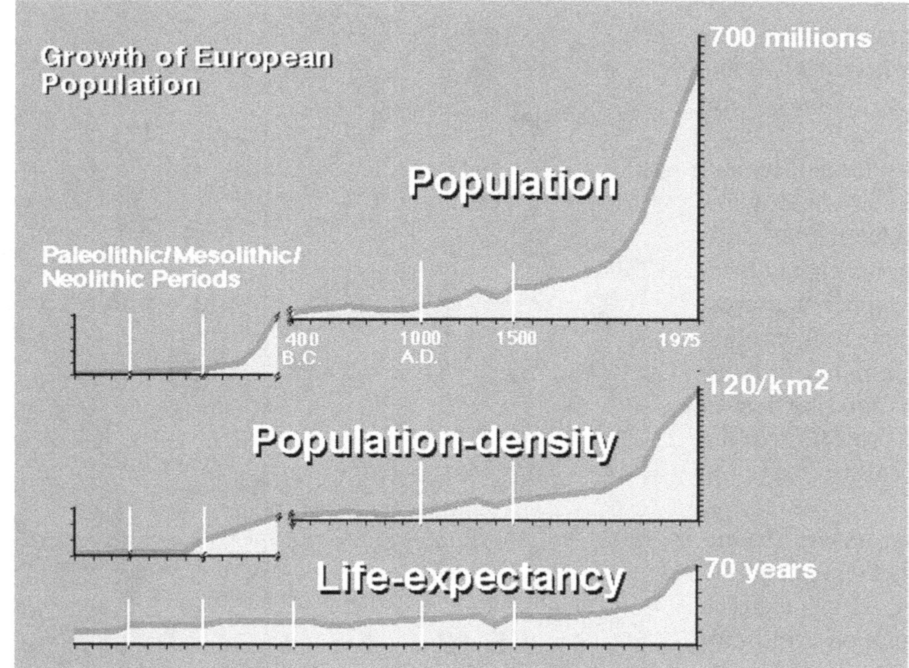

measured per-capita of the society, the more rapid the growth, and the more durable, the profitability and improvement of the conditions of individual life and social relations.

The progress of mankind has depended upon a continuing struggle, to bring society into less imperfect approximation of the requirements of each individual person and total population so gifted, present and future, of the society as a whole. It must be a form of society which fosters, to the maximum practicable degree, that developable cognitive potential which enables students, for example, to become true, adult citizens, rather than merely the degraded, existentialist "subjects" of society: to become the living embodiment of past, present, and future history within themselves, and to accomplish that embodiment through the mental acts of rediscovery of valid principles contributed from the past: developing, thus, the power to generate new, valid principles as solutions to newly defined problems. It must be a form of society which affords each developed individual the opportunity to live in a way which is in accord with that developed cognitive potential.

The struggle to overcome the obstacles to such progress in the human condition, has been a long one, and often a bitter historical process. It is by considering the problems and tasks of modern economy in terms of

historic, and otherwise inferrable pre-historic development, that we are enabled to summon the quality of mind needed to comprehend the efficient connection between progress in social relations, and net increase of the per-capita productive powers of labor.

To that purpose, situate our discussion now, by aid of reference to the most relevant background, to the emergence of those vastly improved forms of social relations, the which were developed through the emergence of national economy and the nation-state republic. We now summarize that case.

After the inevitable, self-imposed decline and ultimate doom of the Empires of Rome and Byzantium, most of the world experienced the beneficial influence of a rise of civilization—a renaissance—in northern India and the Arab world. Toward the end of the millennium, at the point the Arab world was retreating from the high point represented by the Baghdad caliphate of Charlemagne's collaborator, the celebrated Haroun al-Rashid, a new era dawned, both in the Europe whose progress had been preshaped by France's Charlemagne, and with a coincident renaissance in China. The upswing in Europe and China continued until the middle of Europe's Thirteenth Century, ending with a long down-turn, coincident with the effects of the Mongol depredations, throughout vast areas of Eurasia.

Thus, during the middle of the Fourteenth Century, Europe was collapsed into a New Dark Age, after which it rose again, this time into the mid-Fifteenth-Century "Golden Renaissance."[12]

This Fifteenth-Century, Italian Renaissance, centered around the 1439-1440 sessions of the great ecumenical Council of Florence, was reflected in the resulting 1461-1483 reconstitution of France, as the first modern European nation-state, under Louis XI. The same circles in Italy, which organized the Council of

---

12. The same global Eurasian circumstances for the mid-Fifteenth-Century emergence of modern Russia, run parallel to those under which the Italian Renaissance emerged.

Florence and prepared Louis XI's reconstruction of France, designed and promoted the launching of the wave of evangelization toward the lands on the western shores of the Atlantic Ocean, supplying the maps and other relevant instructions used by Christopher Columbus in those voyages of exploration sponsored by Spain's Queen Isabella.[13]

The result of this Fifteenth-Century Italian Renaissance, was the unleashing of the greatest rate of improvement in the productive powers of labor and demographic characteristics of populations, which had been seen in all known human existence. Under this great advance in the human condition, the state took implicit responsibility for fostering the development of the infrastructure of all the nation's territory, and for fostering education, scientific progress, and protection of the improvement and expansion of agriculture, mining, manufactures, and trade.

From the beginning, then, this progress was accomplished in the course of a great struggle to free mankind from those forms of "traditional" society, in which more than ninety percent of the population of all cultures was condemned to live a life of virtual "human cattle," as slaves, serfs, or even worse. In the Mediterranean littoral, and in Europe generally, this was a struggle against a long tradition of what was called the "oligarchical model" of ancient Babylon and Tyre, as continued by Rome and Byzantium, and, as continued under European feudalism.

Therefore, the Fifteenth Century's birth of a new society of freedom and progress, faced bloody reaction from the feudal oligarchy, both from landed aristocracies, and from financial oligarchies of the type represented by the *Phanariots* of Byzantium and by the nobility of a new Tyre, Venice. Man would never be free, until nations were freed from the yoke of the two great feudal parasites, landed aristocracy and Venice-style financier oligarchy. The latter part of that task has yet to be accomplished.

Inevitably, the struggle for establishing the modern form of post-feudal society, made war against Venice's incarnate evil inevitable, and justifiable. The crucial effort to crush Venice, and its succubus-like system of financier-oligarchism, reached a critical juncture, during the first decade of the Sixteenth Century, in the alliance,

Venetian oligarchs go about their dirty dealings in the dead of night (a 1785 engraving). "Inevitably, the struggle for establishing the modern form of post-feudal society, made war against Venice's incarnate evil inevitable, and justifiable."

against Venice, by the France-led League of Cambrai. At the point Venice was about to be crushed, Venice exploited the cupidity of some members of the League, to split them from the League, and, even to become tools of Mephistophelian Venice against France.

Thus, Venice escaped its just defeat, and was able to launch a counteroffensive. Venice split Europe between what became respectively Protestant and Catholic parties, playing both camps against each other. Venice, through such of its operations as its seduction of England's Henry VIII, put the former nation-state allies, France, England, and Spain, at one another's throats, and unleashed the lunacy of religious wars throughout Europe, culminating in that 1618-1648 Thirty Years War which depopulated and ruined every nation of central Europe.

However, despite the effects of Venice's "balance of power" games in religion and politics, the social institutions of the nation-state and national economy, gave the average citizen of the new form of state a per-capita

---

13. The reader should be reminded, that both Louis XI's reconstitution of France, and Columbus' voyages, were the result of initiatives supplied by the circles, around Cardinal Nicolaus of Cusa, associated with the Council of Florence.

strategic advantage in economy and in warfare. As Venice, during the course of the Sixteenth Century, came to recognize these intrinsic strategic advantages of national economy, the leading faction of Venice, headed by Paolo Sarpi, worked to develop both the Netherlands and England as maritime powers ruled by a financier-oligarchical class, making the ruling oligarchies of these nation-states clones and tools of Venice.

In the course of the wars to which this Venetian manipulation of England's and the Netherlands' roles led, during the Seventeenth and Eighteenth Centuries, all of Europe came under the domination of the combination of Venice and the Anglo-Dutch financier-oligarchic maritime powers which were Venice's allies, and, after the close of the Eighteenth Century, became Venice's successors. These successors were known as the "Venetian Party," or, in the alternative, the "Enlightenment" party, of Eighteenth-Century Europe.[14]

In this way, the Europe which emerged from the Napoleonic wars was, predominantly, a Europe in which the emergent new nation-states represented a symbiosis of two intrinsically antagonistic institutions: national economy (as that term would be defined by the German-American Friedrich List), versus politically hegemonic financier-oligarchy. Although the relics of the feudal landed aristocracy persisted in gradually reduced circumstances, even after the Palmerston-directed 1848-1849 revolutions on the continent of Europe, landed aristocracy was being either degraded into virtual museum-pieces, or assimilated, with or without titles retained, into the ranks of a "bourgeois" aristocracy, the Anglo-Dutch model of financier-oligarchy.

The conditional exception was the United States, a fact which, despite all the corruption we have endured here, now as earlier, has been key to the historically exceptional, superior character, and global influence, of our species of constitutional republic, ever since 1789.

Under the shackles of the unfavorable political conditions for the nation-state, which Venice's power imposed upon republican-minded Europe, English, French, Dutch, and German colonists, sought to stage their open fight for truth and justice on a choice of battleground at a relatively safer distance from European wars and tyrannies, in North America.[15] Here, semi-autonomous states, governing themselves under provisions of charters obtained, chiefly, from Stuart monarchs, became the foundation for the subsequent establishment of the first true constitutional republic, the 1789 Federal United States of America, a republic intended to be free of that kind of symbiotic submission to financier-oligarchy which was characteristic of European nations.

Unfortunately, imported fungal spores of the financier-oligarchy also polluted North America, as they did the emerging republics to our South. This so-called "American Tory" corruption persisted, and grew, even after our victory over our mortal enemy, Britain, even after the establishment of our constitutional republic.

Under the unfavorable strategic conditions of the Napoleonic wars and the 1814-1848 power of Britain's alliance with Metternich et al., the United States had no friend, but only enemies, among the foreign governments of note. Foreign meddling into our internal affairs, partly by Metternich's "Holy Alliance,"[16] and chiefly by our deadly enemy, the British Empire, fostered three elements of London-allied financier-oligarchism among us: the New England and other opium-trading partners of the British East India Company; the London-controlled Manhattan bankers, such as the

---

14. On the use of the term "Venetian Party" in England, and elsewhere, during the Seventeenth and Eighteenth Centuries, compare H. Graham Lowry, *How The Nation Was Won* (Washington, D.C.: EIR News Service, 1987), passim. This was otherwise known as the party of philosophical liberalism (e.g., empiricism), or, the same thing, the party of the Seventeenth and Eighteenth Centuries' English and French "Enlightenment," as opposed to Christian and republican values, such as those represented in science by Kepler, William Gilbert, Christiaan Huyghens, Gottfried Leibniz, Moses Mendelssohn, Lessing, and the circles of Benjamin Franklin.

15. There were parallel developments, in opposition to the pervasive oligarchical corruption of the "mother country," in Hispanic Central and South America. Yet, contrary to the chauvinist, anti-Yanqui mythologies rampant in some Ibero-American circles, it was the impact of the "American model," as spread both from the United States, or, as echoed from continental Europe, which gave efficient form of expression to the successful kind of economic development which appeared in Central and South America, during the course of the Nineteenth Century. Indeed, the "American model" was the key to every form of economic and related social progress experienced in Eurasia, Australia, or the Americas as a whole.

16. The principal Holy Alliance operations against the U.S.A. during the 1814-1848 interval, were either directed through the Habsburg-dominated (e.g., Metternich) Austro-Hungarian, Spanish, and Portuguese channels in the Caribbean and South America region, or in conjunction with the British monarchy. This continued to be a significant problem for U.S. security through the end of the U.S. Civil War. These networks contributed a part in the assassination of President Abraham Lincoln. This overlapped the operations conducted against the United States by the family of Napoleon Bonaparte, all of whom became either British Foreign Service, or Metternich agents, after the defeat of Napoleon Bonaparte himself. Notably, it is the family of Napoleon Bonaparte which popularized the neologism "Latin America," as part of the imperious Napoleon III's efforts to grab former Spanish colonies for France's Nineteenth-century "junior empire."

body, unless that body was inalterably wedded, and subordinated to a rapacious parasite, a financier oligarchy of the Anglo-Dutch "Venetian Party" type. Yet, because national economy was strategically indispensable for national defense (and, also, for conquests), each time the oligarchy sucked the national economy into an economic depression, the same oligarchy, for political and strategic reasons, was, sooner or later, compelled to unleash the processes of growth inhering in national economy. This pattern persisted, with some slight modifications, during the years 1901-1964, until the aftermath of détente agreements reached between the Soviet Union and Anglo-American powers, following the 1962 missiles-crisis.

Gen. George Washington reviewing the troops at Valley Forge. The American colonists established the world's first true constitutional republic, intended to be free of that kind of symbiotic submission to financier-oligarchy which was characteristic of European nations.

Bank of Manhattan's Aaron Burr and treasonous August Belmont; and, the southern slaveocracy.

This symbiosis of national economy—primarily in Europe, but also spread into the U.S.A.—under the influence of a parasitical financier oligarchy, is the origin of the so-called "business cycle."

The popularized notion of the business cycle, which was put forward by Britain's Haileybury school, and Karl Marx, during the Nineteenth Century, was, at that time, essentially a British East India Company hoax. The idea that boom-bust cycles are characteristic of modern nation-state economy, was a sophistry employed in defense of the British East India Company's claim,[17] that national economy could not have a healthy

The developments of 1929-1931, and following that, of 1934-1945, are typical of this kind of business cycle. This is also the case with the deep post-war, Truman recession of 1946-1948, the post-Korean War recession of 1952-1954, and the deep recession of 1957-1958. However, the developments of the post-1964 period, to date, do not correspond to what was

---

17. Pro-satanist (*The Theory of the Moral Sentiments*—1759) Adam Smith's 1776 British East India Company propaganda-tract, *The Wealth of Nations*, is merely typical of the same Company's Haileybury School, and of all leading British economists and their admirers since. While, in fact, England and the United Kingdom were passionately protectionist at home, until relatively recent Twentieth-Century changes, they demanded a strict policy of "free trade" from all their intended victims. Smith's *Wealth of Nations*, published on the eve of the U.S. Declaration of Independence, was written at the behest of the notorious Lord Shelburne, as an anti-American and anti-France propaganda tract of Smith's employer, the British East India Company. This book had little influence among American patriots, until the late 1790s period of the U.S.A.'s near-war with Napoleon Bonaparte's France. The disastrous effects of the introduction of "free trade" policies to the U.S.A., by British agent Albert Gallatin, under the administrations of Presidents Thomas Jefferson and Dolley Madison's James, produced the patriotic sense of outrage expressed by such influential writings of Philadelphia's Mathew Carey as his *The Olive Branch* and his celebrated 1819 contributions to *The Addresses of the Philadelphia Society for the Promotion of National Industry* [See Allen Salisbury, *The Civil War and the American System: America's Battle with Britain, 1860-1876* (New York: Campaigner Publications, 1978)]. The German-American Friedrich List was trained under the leadership of Mathew Carey. The policies of Benjamin Franklin, Alexander Hamilton, Mathew Carey, Henry Clay, and John Quincy Adams, were introduced as national economic policy again, under the guidance of Henry C. Carey, during the 1861-1879 interval, lifting the U.S.A. rapidly to the status of the most powerful and most technological advanced industrial economy of the world. Under Henry Carey's influence, these policies were introduced, during that latter period, to Meiji Restoration Japan, Germany, and Russia, among other nations of the world. What Hamilton, the Careys, and List, among others, defined as the anti-British, anti-"free trade," "American System of political-economy," is the original historical model of modern national economy as such, world wide.

A 1777 cartoon shows "Poor old England endeavoring to reclaim wicked American children." Unfortunately, writes LaRouche, "imported fungal spores of the financier-oligarchy also polluted North America, as they did the emerging republics to our South."

formerly defined as a "business cycle."

The difference with the world after 1964, is, that the occasion of the establishment of a process of "détente" between the world's two leading nuclear power-blocs, was seen by the modern heirs of the Seventeenth and Eighteenth Centuries' "Venetian Party," as ending the likelihood of Classical modern warfare, and thus limiting future wars to what are termed alternately "limited," or "cabinet warfare," such as the Vietnam War, "surrogate warfare," and what is best described as "irregular warfare."[18] The designation "irregular warfare," includes the use of terrorist organizations as controlled surrogates of such powers as the world's leading patron of international terrorism today, the British monarchy.[19] Notably, exemplary "moles" pushing for this change from within the Kennedy and Johnson administrations, were the prominent authors of the U.S.' mid-1960s Vietnam War: Defense Secretary Robert McNamara and Henry A. Kissinger patron and National Security Advisor McGeorge Bundy.

Under these conditions of a "détente process" modelled upon the doctrines of Bertrand Russell[20] and the Pugwash Conference,[21] the financier-oligarchic factions unleashed a campaign to undermine, ultimately to eliminate national economy from the planet Earth.[22] The campaign began during the middle 1960s, although the openly avowed commitment to elimination of the existence of nation-states waited, until the 1989-1990 onset of the collapse of former Soviet power, and President George Bush's promulgation of Mrs. Thatcher's doctrine of "globalization," Bush's "new world order."

The initial, mid-1960s attacks upon the institutions of the nation-state, and against continued investment in fundamental scientific progress, were focussed upon the generation of youth entering universities during the middle to late 1960s. The initial concentration of the "rock-drug-sex youth-counterculture," "information society," "post-industrial" utopianism, and, beginning late 1969, "ecologism," was concentrated upon these culturally pessimistic, "shell-shocked" victims of the missile-crisis, Kennedy assassination, and nightly Vietnam TV shows. The target of this focus was the stratum which

---

18. E.g., the surrogate war launched in Afghanistan beginning 1979. The term "Classical" signifies warfare as defined by Lazare Carnot's 1792-1794 reforms of the French army and national economy for victory over the invading armies of France's enemies. This ended, for a time at least, that feudal tradition in warfare otherwise known, during the Eighteenth Century, as "cabinet warfare:" war as a weapon left in the hands of diplomacy. Essentially, under "cabinet warfare" rules, the military were liveried lackeys sent to administer a few bloody beatings to "soften up the other side" for the demands of the diplomats. "Classical" warfare, by contrast, was designed (as the "Schlieffen Plan" and U.S.A. policy for World War II illustrate this) to annihilate the adversaries' capability and will to continue effective organized war-fighting. The so-called "U.S. War in Vietnam" was designed and conducted as a feudalistic "cabinet warfare" from inception to end, degrading the U.S. military from the army of a modern republic, to a bunch of "uglies in livery," deployed as gangsters' hit-men.

19. See **EIR** series: "The New International Terrorism," Oct. 13, 1995; "London's Irregular Warfare vs. Nations of the Americas," Nov. 10, 1995; "RIM: London's Narco-Terrorist International," Nov. 17, 1995.

20. Bertrand Russell, "The Atomic Bomb and the Prevention of War," **Bulletin of the Atomic Scientists**, Nos. 5 and 6, Sept. 1, 1946, p. 19.

21. Lyndon H. LaRouche, Jr., "How Bertrand Russell Became an Evil Man," **Fidelio**, Fall 1994, pp. 4-75.

22. This was the "one-world" policy long associated with Bertrand Russell, H.G. Wells, the World Federalists, and the present-day World Council of Churches. The nuclear policy introduced to U.S. strategic doctrine by Britain's Russell, was first developed by H.G. Wells on the basis of Frederick Soddy's pre-World War I showing of the feasibility of both nuclear weapons and nuclear power.

would rise into top positions of government, education, business, and the learned professions, over the course of a coming generation—or, the authors of this "New Age" brainwashing of our youth hoped, "degeneration."

In summary, the effect was to bring about a turn away from investment in both basic economic infrastructure, and scientific and technological progress, and, to introduce coordinate changes in education, in wages-policy, and in social-welfare policies. If we take into account the attrition suffered by prior investments in infrastructure and production, and if we measure the "energy-of-the-system" content of relevant producer and household market-baskets in physical content, the U.S. economy has been contracting, in physical economy's "energy of the system" terms, per job, per capita of labor-force, at rates in excess of 2% per annum, each year, since 1970-1971.[23]

This long-term trend of net negative investment in the physical productivity of the U.S. economy, has provided the margin of negative accumulation of wealth, the which has been used to generate nominal financial profits of enterprises in the economy. The discounting of this marginal negative investment, has provided that flow of funds from the Federal Reserve System, which has been used, increasingly, to leverage financial capital gains in fictitious assets, rather than fostering real investment in production of wealth. Since 1971, speculation against "floating" national currencies, in "Petrodollar" loans, in "Junk Bonds," and in the form of casino-gambling called "derivatives," has vir-

A demonstration in New York City in 1980. Victims of the counterculture's "New Age" brainwashing, have now risen to the top positions in government and other institutions.

tually superseded real investment with purely fictitious, leveraged financial gains, as a source of nominal financial profit.[24]

Then, as referenced above, in 1989, the cabal of Britain's Prime Minister Margaret Thatcher, France's President François Mitterrand, and U.S. President George Bush, combined forces, to announce the coming end of the existence of the modern nation-state, and the beginning of a "one-world" utopia, a "globalized" nightmare, President Bush's "new world order."

The impetus for this policy, as for the war against Iraq, came from Prime Minister Thatcher's government. This was introduced in Autumn 1989, under the banner of a racialist, Thatcher hate-campaign against Germans. The propaganda-campaign for the British government's devolutionist policy against continental Europe, was led by a pair of scoundrels, Conor Cruise O'Brien and Mrs. Thatcher's Minister Nicholas Ridley. In this matter, Mrs. Thatcher was served by France's regrettable President, British agent of anti-De Gaulle influence, François Mitterrand.

Thatcher and Mitterrand intended to prevent the reunification of Germany, arguing that a more powerful German "d-Mark" would establish Germany as a men-

---

23. A technical note is required here: By "energy of the system" terms, we signify the assigning of the index-value "1.000" to that array of market-baskets of infrastructure, agriculture, industry, households, and professional scientific services, which is required to maintain the productive equipotential of the national economy and its population as a unit-whole. All of these market-baskets must be taken into account, per capita of labor-force, and per square kilometer of relevant land-area, in estimating the content of them all required to maintain the effective equipotential of national-economic, physical productivity per capita. This equipotential, which corresponds to a constant standard of value for "potential relative population-density," is the level of per-capita physical output, measured in per-capita market-basket terms for each and all of the indicated household and other categories, per capita, which is necessary to maintain, or improve the ratio of "free energy" to "energy of the system," under the included condition, that the density of the "energy of the system" must increase, in order to foster the rates of technological progress upon which such minimal standards of ratio of "free energy" to "energy of the system" depend.

24. Lowering the capital-gains tax-rate, to favor such parasitical speculation, at the expense of the real economy, has been part of this "post-industrial" orgy of national economic lunacy.

acing "Fourth Reich." When President Bush was persuaded by advisors that this would not be a smart move, a compromise was struck among Thatcher, Mitterrand, and Bush, to force the German government to pledge to destroy a unified Germany's economy and national sovereignty piece-meal, as a precondition for allowing the reunification of Germany under the terms of extant "Four Power" agreements. The imposition of this economic suicide-pact upon Germany, was part of the same process by which the former Soviet allies of eastern Europe and the Soviet Union itself, would be looted systematically, and savagely, to the point of virtual extinction.

Under a rampage of "free trade" policies and practices, the world's physical economy has been collapsed to the breaking-point. In such a manner, Mrs. Thatcher's handshake jerked President Bush into the 1990-1991 "Desert Storm" war against Iraq. Thus, Britain and Mitterrand's France unleashed a new Balkan war in what they stated to be their aim to "contain the German economy's growth," a London-directed war, using British and French Balkan puppets and other assets, which was intended to destroy the economy and nations of all Balkan countries, for a long time to come. Thus, the self-destruction of the economy of western Europe, and the IMF-dictated destruction of the economies and peoples of eastern Europe, including the former Soviet Union, has proceeded apace.

Thus, the British-directed, willful self-destruction of western continental Europe, and the IMF-dictated destruction of the economies of eastern Europe and the former Soviet Union, have continental Europe qualifying itself economically for associate membership, among the victims of, chiefly, British imperialism, in the "Association of Looted African States" (ALAS).

Meanwhile, the success of the "summit" between President Clinton and Jiang Zemin, over the objections of the "loyal British opposition" inside the U.S. Congress and in Tory Hollywood, has completed the process of shifting the center of political-economic gravity of our planet, away from the Atlantic crossing, to the transit of goods and technology across the Pacific and Indian oceans.

However, despite the success of that "summit," the collapse of the world economy, aggravated by the "Venetian Party's" speculative raids against both the currencies and economies of East and Southeast Asia, of Africa, and Central and South America, has already detonated the potential for a bottomless collapse of the world's entire financial and monetary system.

In the meantime, since the developments of 1988-1990, the biggest, most burstable bubble in history, has been built up, as an accumulation of virtual "casino side-bets" against the ashes of the ruined former national economies of Europe, Africa, and the Americas. The total current obligations of the international financial system, are presently several times the current GDP of all nations combined: every banking system on this planet, with the possible exception of China's, is hopelessly bankrupt, if current accounts were to be reconciled. There is no bottom to this ongoing financial crisis, and there is only a fraction of the physical economy which the world once had, to be mobilized in the effort to build a new, viable financial and monetary system. We have entered fully into the maelstrom; we are now enjoying the terminal phase of a systemic crisis, a crisis which absolutely ensures the end of the system, probably before the end of the century, possibly much sooner.

Thus, we have entered, not a boom-depression-cycle's collapse, but a disintegration of the financial system of a virtual "post-industrial" society.

At the same time, this collapse-process intersects the implications of the Clinton-Jiang Zemin summit: the only hope for building a revival of world economy, out of the ashes of an unstoppable, bottomless collapse of the old financial-monetary system, now depends upon building bridges around the pivot of cooperation between the U.S.A. and China. The kind of world which could be rebuilt from the ruin of this bottomless financial debacle, this collapse now entering its terminal phases, must include the most populous nations of East and South Asia, as partners with the U.S.A., and must also include those nations of Europe, including Russia, which are willing to commit themselves strategically to this partnership built around cooperation between the U.S.A. and China.

The Curvature of Economic Physical Space-Time

We have reached the point in this report, at which to address directly the paradox-ridden topic: *Whence do we derive the mathematical expressions which arise out of measuring selected results of social relations?*

Primarily, the paradox is this. Since the actions which we call "productive," are each and all expressed as physical actions upon nature, how is it possible, that all successful forms of society, are mathematically anti-entropic in their ordering, rather than of that entropic form, the which generally accepted types of modern statistical methods attribute to all kinds of interactions among, or with non-living physical processes?[25] *Whence the source of that anti-entropic physical-space-time curvature, the which is characteristic of all societies characterized by net improvement of the productivities, per-capita standard of living, and demographic characteristics of the households, of the population considered as a unit-whole?*[26]

An adequate solution for this challenge, is supplied by focussing upon two specific contributions to physical science and knowledge in general, from among those of Gottfried Leibniz and Bernhard Riemann. The first, in historical sequence, is the notion of the *monad*, as supplied by Leibniz. The second, is Riemann's replacement of the earlier, flawed notions, those of matter interacting algebraically within a linearized Euclidean space-time geometry, replacing this mechanistic schema by the notion of *a general theory of physical-space-time manifolds*. The first, Leibniz's notion of the monad, locates the efficient source of functionally anti-entropic curvature occurring within the physical mac-roeconomic domain. The second, Riemann's general theory of manifolds, enables us to show, and implicitly to measure, the changes in curvature which are characteristic of productive, or functionally related activity, under conditions of realized scientific and technological progress.

We begin this phase of our report with the second case, the implication of *orderable systems of Riemannian manifolds*.

The notion of any Riemannian manifold, is best comprehended, by reference to the system of Plato's Socratic dialogues taken as a whole, with notable included emphasis upon the exemplary *Parmenides*. The most crucial notions to be so adduced, respecting the underlying principles of an orderable system of successive Riemannian manifolds, are Plato's notions of *hypothesis, higher hypothesis, Becoming,* and *Good*.

As Riemann himself has stressed this fact, the crucial conception, upon which the barest notion of a Riemannian manifold depends absolutely, is Plato's notion of *hypothesis*.[27] The simplest form of hypothesis, is any set of interacting definitions, axioms, and postulates, upon which the existence of a corresponding set of theorems depends.

In its simplest expression, this notion of hypothesis implies a deductive relationship of non-inconsistency between any acceptable theorem of the system, and each and all of the terms of the underlying hypothesis of such a theorem-lattice. However, the reader must be warned, that this is not limited to the case of deductive theorem-lattices. We include higher-order manifolds, such as those "metamathematical" ("modular," "hyper-geometric") types of non-linear manifolds which, as Leibniz warned, can not be adequately defined within the confines of algebraic deductive relations.[28]

Provided that a real existence is demonstrated (e.g., experimentally) for the proposition considered, and that the proposition is not inconsistent with any of the terms of the underlying hypothesis, the proposition qualifies as a theorem of the theorem-lattice defined by that specific hypothesis.

---

25. This paradox is key to understanding the essentially anti-scientific method employed to construct or defend all of the popularized "ecological" dogmatism of the recent twenty-five-odd years. All of the arguments made by the spokesmen for this irrationalist cult, when they are not simple lying, depend upon the kinds of assumptions central to "linear computer models" of the type associated with F. Sherwood Rowland's contribution to fabricating the "Ozone Hole" hoax, and the related models upon which the "Global Warming" hoax is premised. The use of any computer or analogous mathematical model, is a linear "curve-fitting" form of mathematical construction, which axiomatically delimits the functional representations to entropic ones. Like all of the leading modern arguments for the assumption that nature is axiomatically linear in the very small (e.g., infinitesimal), the mathematical models employed by today's "ecologists" are intrinsically frauds, hoaxes which are based on the fallacy called *petitio principii*: the conclusion reached by calculation, was embedded as an axiom of the construction before the first step of the calculation was begun. Since the growth of human population is based on cultures which have the relatively highest rate of anti-entropy in their relationship to nature in general, the axiomatic assumption of all the typical "ecologist" models is fraudulent on principle.

26. Here lies the key to understanding the absurdity of that fascist conceit, the myth of so-called "artificial intelligence," better named "digital virtual man." This cult was perpetrated in its present form by radical positivists such as MIT's Norbert Wiener, John von Neumann, MIT's Marvin Minsky, et al. (Statistical "information theory" is, axiomatically, the same fraud as the notion of "artificial intelligence.") How were it feasible, to construct an apparatus, which by design, was incapable of any action inconsistent with linearity in the infinitesimal, and, yet, propose that it would be distinguished by its ability to perform operations which are intrinsically anti-entropic! There are few celebrated scientific hoaxes in history which were not premised on fraud of the same types as "information theory."

27. Bernhard Riemann, *Über die Hypothesen, welche der Geometrie zu Grunde liegen* ("On the Hypotheses which Underlie Geometry"), in **Bernhard Riemanns gesammelte mathematische Werke**, H. Weber, ed. (New York: Dover Publications reprint, 1953).

28. E.g., "*Analysis Situs.*" Classical musical thorough-composition, of the type which Wolfgang Mozart and his successors, through Johannes Brahms, derived from pioneering achievements by Johann Sebastian Bach, is an example of such a manifold.

Riemannian manifolds are characteristically of the higher, non-linear order of hypothesis. Any Riemannian physical-space-time manifold has two general characteristics, which distinguish it absolutely from the Euclid-like manifolds of algebra.

First, the existence of self-evident forms of definitions, axioms, and postulates, is banned absolutely. In particular, all "self-evident" notions of *extension*, *action*, or *continuity* are absolutely excluded. No presumption which claims to bound the action within a manifold, or a system of manifolds, by deduction, is permitted. All of the dimensions of a manifold, such as the notions of extension in space and time, exist only to the degree they have a basis for existence as experimentally demonstrable, efficient principles, in the sense of principle supplied by the Socratic dialectic's notion of *Platonic ideas*.

Second, as Riemann stresses most heavily, most notably in the concluding portion of his habilitation dissertation,[29] we can not consider the "dimensions" of a manifold to be thoroughly independent of one another. As the nature of *Analysis Situs* illustrates this fact, the dimensions of a Riemannian manifold interact, to the effect of determining an internal, characteristic, "curvature" of the manifold, which we are obliged to adduce by relevant crucial experimentation, rather than from relying upon an assumed, formal, relative independence of each of the dimensions of that physical-space-time manifold being considered.

Within the bounds of the physical-science curriculum, the notion of an ordered succession of Riemannian manifolds confronts the student, in each case a previously demonstrated system of physics-knowledge is overturned by experimental validation of a new physical principle (or, in the alternative, what is for the student, at that moment, at least, a new physical principle). The required addition of the new principle to the hypothesis of the challenged manifold, produces a new manifold, with what are usually accompanying differences between the crucially demonstrable, characteristic curvature of the new manifold, and that of the superseded manifold.[30] Thus, physical science presents an elementary demonstration of the way in which at least one type of series of manifolds may be ordered.[31]

Examining this matter more closely, brings us to a direct encounter with Leibniz's notion of the *monad*. Looking at science and technology from the standpoint of the development of the modern principle of machine-tool design, since Lazare Carnot's introduction of this, we encounter that feature of Riemannian manifolds which leads our attention back to Leibniz's original notions of *Analysis Situs* and *monad*.

As stated in the Bad Godesberg address, and other locations earlier, the beginning of the discovery and economic application of new physical principle, is best described in terms of four essential, sequential steps. The proof of the existence and significance of the *monad*, is located in reflection upon the second of those four steps. These steps are as follows.

The first step, is the confrontation of an established, experimentally validated, or other mathematical physics, by experimentally validatable evidence of the existence of effects which that established mathematical physics implicitly prohibits. The impact of W. Weber's experimental proof of the Ampère-Weber "longitudinal force" of electrodynamics, to the effect of implicitly overturning the electrodynamics of Maxwell, is an excellent example of this step.[32]

Since, the best claims of the old physics, and the contrary claims of the newly considered physical evidence, are premised upon the same faculty of demonstration, the two claims are *ontologically* counterposed, as, in this degree, mutually exclusive. The old physics and the new evidence, do not inhabit the same universe.

---

29. Op. cit., p. 287. concluding sentence.

30. One of the pedagogically best illustrations of this difference, is found in the history of the experimental proof, by Gauss's and Riemann's collaborator, Wilhelm Weber, of the Ampère-Weber "longitudinal force" of electrodynamics, which requires abandoning the popular delusion that the so-called "Coulomb Force" simply governs physical relations within the region of smallness bounding the atomic nucleus.

The physical-space-time curvature of the manifold incorporating Weber's proof, differs in this way, and others, from the manifold simply defined by James C. Maxwell.

31. Everything which is said of the discovery of validatable solutions to ontological paradoxes from the domain of physical science, applies to the role of the form of ontological paradox called "metaphor" in Classical art-forms. In the latter case, the validatable solutions generated, in response to metaphor, within the individual mind, are ideas of the same formal type as discovered validatable solutions of physical principle in physical science. The difference is, that physical science addresses man's interaction with the physical universe, whereas Classical art-forms address both the principles of the mind, by means of which the physical discoveries of principle are effected, and also the functionally related kinds of relations among persons, as these ideas of Classical art bear upon the social ordering of changes in society's relationship to nature.

32. See Laurence Hecht, "The Significance of the 1845 Gauss-Weber Correspondence," *21st Century Science & Technology*, Fall 1996.

This is the prototype of what we term, in Classical epistemology, an *ontological paradox*. Plato's *Parmenides* provides the exemplary definition of "ontological paradox" as a cognitive type. Since the universe is real, it must be presumed that the old physics is that which has abandoned citizenship in the real universe.

These types of ontological paradoxes are the prompting for all human creativity, and of willful progress of all kinds in the human condition. These types of ontological paradoxes, are what defines the absolute difference between man and beast, or man and robot. The ability of the individual human mind, to generate validatable notions of principle, by means of which these ontological paradoxes are solved, is the site of that agency of human cognition, the which is the provable quality defining the human individual as possessed of a characteristic "divine spark of Reason," as "man in the image of God."

In the second step, these powers of cognition are aroused by a passion to generate a solution, in the form of discovered principle, for the ontological paradox presented. In the case, that the individual succeeds in this cognitive enterprise, *no external observer can see, hear, touch, or smell, the specific act by which the discovered principle is generated in the mind of the discoverer*. The only way in which that individual's act can be verified as occurring, is through the replication of the same accomplishment, in the same way, by another person. There is no other way, except replication, by means of which the *act* of discovery *itself* can be known. Demonstrably efficient concepts which have the basis for their existence as discovered notions of this type, represent the class of notions, external to direct sense-perception, which are known as *Platonic ideas*.

This is the heart of what is properly referenced by the term "Platonic Realism." The physical universe is demonstrably ordered by efficient principles which can not be identified in the form of sense-perceptions, even though their efficiency, as fully existent principles, is demonstrated empirically—e.g., by means of "crucial," proof-of-principle experiments. Thus, in discovering such validated principles, we are uncovering, as existent within the domain of Platonic ideas, fully efficient principles of the universe, principles which determine the manner in which the perceptible events expressed by that universe are ordered. Thus, the domain of such principles, is the domain of reality, whereas, the domain of sense-perception, by itself, without knowledge of such Platonic ideas—the world of TV's "Sergeant Joe Friday," and his, "Just the facts, Ma'am"—is a shadow-world, in which men and women are the hapless victims of those irrational, inhuman cruelties which are the harvest of ignorant superstitions.

Unlike the results of the second step, the posing of the ontological paradox, in the first step, was *representable* in modes of communication which make use of sense-perception. However, the ideas themselves can not be contained within such a language or other mode of communication as such. Hence, the obvious hoax in Wiener's dogma of "information theory."

This carries us to *the third step*. The person who has discovered the notion of a principle which he thinks has solved the paradox, may now represent the effect of that discovery in terms of the statement of the paradox in step one. This statement is expressed in a way which implies some proof-of-principle demonstration of the actual efficiency of the discovered principle: this shadow-form of the act of discovery is *representable*.

The next, *fourth step*, is the designing, conducting, and so forth, of the proof-of-principle experiment. As soon as proof-of-principle has been experimentally validated, the experimental apparatus itself becomes a point of reference for designing new kinds of products, and new kinds of productive processes, in which the newly discovered physical principle is incorporated to advantage. This fourth step, thus defines the surface of interface between fundamental scientific research, and production, an interface more easily recognized by the name "machine-tool-design" sector of a national economy.

It should not be necessary to reconstruct, from the beginning, the obvious fact, that this relationship, between that quality of the individual person represented by the second step, and the effect of discovery, expresses the characteristic distinction of "human." This quality of the individual's developable, cognitive processes, is the persisting point of origin of all successful economy, whether that individual is acting as a scientist, or employed as productive labor assimilating scientific and technological progress into the process of production.

"Where do we find this most characteristic, determining principle of economy reflected, among the textbooks and classrooms of the university?"

Essentially, today, nowhere!

"Where is this principle found in the serf looted by François Quesnay's lordly *laissez-faire*, in Adam Smith, in Karl Marx,[33] and so on? Where is it in the formulation of the policies which have misshaped the U.S.A. economy during the recent thirty-odd years? Where is it in the deliberations of the U.S. Congress today? What neo-conservative, a professed 'evangelical' or not, is willing to replace his obsessive reliance on old lusty witches' 'magic of the marketplace,' by an economy designed for human beings each made in the image of God?"

From the vantage-point of physics, as it was for Gottfried Leibniz, economy is an essential expression of the relationship between the continued existence of the human species as a whole, and the universe as a whole. Thus, real economy can not be other than physical economy, and real profit can be nothing other than an expression of the increase of the potential relative population-density, the *functional* physical standard of living, and improvement of the *functional* demographic characteristics, of each of the totality of households of which the total population and its reproduction are composed.

This unique quality of relationship between mankind as a whole, and the universe as a whole, is located in those changes which the realization of humanly discovered principles imposes upon the universe around us. These changes are generated within what we have described as "the second step" of the process of generating a validatable new discovery of a principle of nature itself, including the Classical-artistic principles of those mental processes (cognition) by means of which these discoveries are effected.

---

33. This was the central feature of my one-semester university lectures, of 1966-1973, in my course on Marx's economics, in distinguishing between the results of Marx's view and my own; I have neither changed my position, nor needed to, since then, to the present date. In Marx's ***Capital*** I, and elsewhere, he warns the reader that he is leaving the "technological composition of capitals" out of account. Although, in other locations in the three volumes of ***Capital*** and ***Theories of Surplus Value***, Marx takes into account the impact of technology upon price-changes, nowhere does he recognize the standpoint of Leibnizian physical economy, that what Marx puts aside, anti-entropic implications of his omitted "technological composition of capitals," determines physical-economic "value," even though, in a related matter, he rejects Lassalle's "iron law of wages" with sound argument. On the related issue, the dominant role of finance-oligarchy in British Eighteenth-century political-economy, Marx tends, predominantly, to the mistaken view, that this social-political class is an integral feature of modern national economy. Hence, the fallacy of his model of "extended reproduction" and his mistaken attribution of the origins of "internal contradictions" of capital. To the best of my knowledge, Marx is the only successor of the British East India Company's school, who acknowledges the fact of omission of the "technological composition of capitals."

We do not *know* the universe from the standpoint of an objective observer contemplating the evidence. We *know* the universe only in terms of discovered, efficient principles of change, changes of that quality which is expressed as an ordered succession of Riemannian manifolds. We know this best in terms of what Gauss and Riemann define as those principles of "curvature" to which I made reference, in contrasting a cyclical economic crisis to the presently terminal, systemic breakdown of the present international financial system.

We have two instances of curvatures to consider. On the one hand, we have the changes in curvature which correspond to progress in the series of manifolds typified by advances in efficient human knowledge. On the other hand, we have the changing curvature of that orderable set of manifolds, the which corresponds to the advancement of man's practice upon the universe. It is the correspondence between the two curvatures, which some might prefer we distinguish as "subjective" and "objective," respectively, which ought to be considered as of the greatest importance for a valid science of physical economy.

In other words, we have the changing "curvature" represented by the self-development of that *monad*, as expressed in step two, above, which is the essence of the individual person. We have also, the changing "curvature" of adduced physical space-time, corresponding to fundamental scientific advances in human practice upon the universe at large. The question is, how are these two—"subjective" and "objective"—related?

The feature of most immediate importance for us, as human beings, is the specific curvature of mankind's successful relationship, as a species, to the universe as a whole. This curvature is specifically *anti-entropic*:

> the requirement that the ratio of *physical-economic free energy* to *physical-economic energy of the system,* be *positive*, and that this ratio not decline, under the added condition that this result demands the *functionally increasing density of physical-economic energy of the system*, both *per capita of labor-force*, and *per square kilometer of relevant surface area*. This desired curvature is sustained solely through emphasis upon investment of society's allocable resources in the equivalent, and correlatives, of scientific and technological progress.

That functionally defined curvature corresponds to

an ordered succession of Riemannian manifolds, as we have situated the four-step process. This four-step process is driven by the mental processes which also describe an ordered succession of Riemannian manifolds, as we have indicated that here. This complementarity of functionally determined ordering, defines an axiomatically hypergeometric type of anti-entropic function, this located within the domain which Leibniz identifies by "*Analysis Situs.*" Soon, below, we shall return to Plato's notion of hypothesis, to discover what all this means.

The Human Mind Is Beautiful

Turn attention now, to both the emotional and the intellectual difficulties which, today, most commonly prevent the individual from understanding the principle at issue in this report, difficulties which impel the individual into that obsessive state of economic illiteracy, which has permitted the present state of ongoing collapse of the existing world civilization. We must begin by searching out that adversary, in those most homely precincts of religion, where he, like the monkey, sleeps at night; here is where the relevant, pathological quality of passion makes its dirty nests.

The problems which obstruct the way to understanding those implications of curvature, those which we have just outlined, are rooted in a kind of pathological belief whose typical habitat is popular, especially so-called "low church" varieties of religions and paganist cults. If you leave untouched the obsessions associated with those religious and related beliefs, you will make little headway in bringing rationality into the domain of public, secular matters.

Since the United States, to which this report is principally addressed, is nominally a Christian nation by virtue of the best part of its cultural heritage, if we wish to bring forth the deepest expression of the relevant passions among our readers, we must couch them in the terms in which our subject-matter touches the elementary issues of religious belief.

One of the most crucial, most deadly internal threats to the security of the U.S. today, is the danger expressed by some U.S. theologians, when they err, axiomatically, contrary to Christianity, by insisting that man, by his nature, is "a wretch." If they are consistent, such theologians must imagine that their god, whoever he, she, it, or them, might be, is blind, and entirely lacking in good taste and judgment. Otherwise, why would that god, or gods, spend so much effort, so tirelessly, to woo and succor creatures which these theologians allege to be the most less-than-worthless, most ferally ungrateful creatures one might imagine in this universe. Confronted with such a paradox, a Christian theologian might but throw up his hands, shrug his shoulders, and murmur, "It is a great mystery."

That priest would be mistaken; there is no "great mystery." It is that theologian of wretchedness, not Christ's God, who is deceived. The human species is the best thing in this universe, the only creature with the qualifications to be the companion of the Creator.

The day-by-day problem posed by such speculations, is, that most of our fellow-citizens have yet to grow up. Most continue to be very naughty children, who have not grown up sufficiently, spiritually, to become fully human yet, even at retirement age, although the potential to mature morally, as well as physically, is within our given nature. If we examine more closely those theologians who declare all persons, other than themselves, to be "a wretch like me," it requires little effort to discover, that their fascination with those lusts they call "sinful," is a reflection of their own passion for the same practices which they cite as evidence of other people's, alleged, quality of wretchedness. There is a smell of a doctrine of *laissez-faire* for sin, in their thundering homilies on the subject of other peoples' alleged wretchedness. Something in the mind of the reflective man in the pew, might be overheard to murmur: "If I am the 'low dog' which that real-life 'Elmer Gantry' accuses me of being, then I can not prevent myself from practicing these lusts called 'sin.'"

"Hypocrite" is much too neutral a term, these days, for such theologians of wretchedness. "Pornographer" would be a good choice of generic label. A theologian's declaration of mankind's universal and innate wretchedness, is not a war against sin, but, rather a plea to legalize it. "I could not do otherwise, don't you see; it is in my nature, as a wretched creature. God loves me, you see, because he pities me so much, on account of my enslavement to the lusts of the wretched."

One begins to suspect, that that theologian's image of his god, is really of a British Victorian middle-class lady, perhaps a reader of Dickens, a "Lady-do-Nicely" who spends some hours each week, showing the Irish poor of London how to tat doilies for their table (if the poor can afford one on British wages), and curtains for the windows of their barren dwelling.

In any case, among such theologians, "morality" extends not much further than family matters: such a theologian would never be so immoral as to bring his pros-

President George Bush with Britain's Queen Elizabeth II, in Washington, D.C. May 14, 1991. The British- Israelites have spread the fairy-tale, that the Queen is the lineal descendant of Israel's King David, and thus the rightful ruler of the world.

titute home with him, or, ever wish to be caught doing anything nasty, if that might do injury to the sensibilities of the community on which he relies for a good opinion of himself. If that theologian is caught in the act, doing something nasty, he feigns pitiable contriteness, but expresses this in that slyly threatening way, which says, "After all, are we not all wretches?"

Who is this wretch, which such theologians such as Pat Robertson insist themselves to be? He is, essentially, a caretaker, ministering to the squire's herd of virtual "human cattle." "Elmer Gantry's" typical gull is, after all, the "Yahoo" of Swift's *Gulliver's Travels*. Swift had a clear understanding of the British oligarchy, who, in their own way, have a certain sensibility respecting such matters of statecraft.

The informed British view regards this theological babble about "wretchedness," as characteristic of "low church" religion. Among the sensible, this is rightly understood to signify a variety of religion which has been fabricated, as part of the program for controlling the lower classes, those whose rightful status—in the eyes of the oligarchy, of course—veers toward the serf-like condition of "human cattle."

Since the earliest pagan pantheons, the slicker sort of oligarch has recognized the advantage to the oligarchical system, of insisting that each legalized form of

religions—like the modernist pagan religions of Brigadier Dr. John Rawlings Rees, called psychology and sociology— serve as a measure of social control over the empire's subject populations. Hence, the famous conflict, at Nicea, between the imperial Pontifex Maximus Constantine, and the Christians, was a conflict arising precisely out of the Emperor Constantine's determination to maintain the tradition of Babylon: that each religion legalized to occupy a place in the imperial pagan pantheon, be "adjusted" to serve more conveniently the administrative functions of the empire.

The "low church" doctrines of a Robertson, et al., bear the hallmarks of that Babylonian pantheonic tradition. The particular function for British "low church" designer cults, was as beliefs consistent with the intent to assist the social control over the British Commonwealth's lower classes. This was extended to take in as many credulous U.S. citizens as could be induced to accept the British-Israelite's so-called "evangelical" fairy-tale, that Queen Elizabeth II is currently the lineal descendant of Israel's King David, and thus the rightful ruler of the world. The "evangelical's" genealogical table might be suspect, but the purpose is very much in the real world.

A study of the political effect of such cults as Pat Robertson's, shows, that this blending of pagan magic with a dictionary nominalist's fairy-tale versions of Biblical Prophecy, is designed for no different end in view, than organizing the political and economic stampedes, and other manipulations, of those intended "human cattle" whom the British oligarchy deems "the lower classes." These are classes which the oligarchy prefers would follow the Manichean and Bogomil cults, to receive the misery of their aging years, as just, if cruel, reward for a wretch's unsuitability to receive the mortal gratifications of great wealth and power.

The British variety of "low church,"[34] takes care of

---

34. Naturally, carefully administered by the religious-affairs division

such matters, not only in the United Kingdom and British—or, should we say "Brutish"—Commonwealth, but also exerts top-down control over these cults inside Pat Robertson's U.S.A.

If you wish to smoke out one of those British fellows who specialize in handling the low-church types, merely mention to the suspect, the proposition, that all men and women are born with the gift of a "Divine Spark of Reason": that will set most of them to clambering around the chandelier! If the suspect is too sly to be trapped easily into such a revealing snit, he might simply insist, *adagio sostenuto*, "There is no divine spark of reason," adding, with a measured touch of menace, "you should not be spreading such ideas about."

This banning of the notion, from low-church theology, of man and woman as made in the image of God, echoes the essential features of the doctrines of such Paolo Sarpi assets as England's Francis Bacon, and of such other Sarpi followers as Hobbes, Mandeville, Quesnay, Hume, Adam Smith, Jeremy Bentham, John Locke, and our own native pestilence, pragmatists such as William James and John Dewey. The banning of metaphor, and virtual banning of the Classical subjunctive, from English usage, by Thomas Hobbes' ***Leviathan***, etc., is the essential characteristic of British empiricism and of the Franco-Austrian logical positivism of Norbert Wiener, John von Neumann, et al., after it.

In summary of the crucial burden of these several preceding paragraphs on "low church" matters, the habit of regarding the existence of the second step in our four-step array, as virtually, or absolutely non-existent, is pervasive. That empiricist delusion lurks, waiting to destroy the "divine spark of humanity," from the low-church pulpit, as in the economics classroom, and every other place where the Orwellian nightmares called "mainstream opinion" reign today. It is ironical, that an efficient notion of the soul, is driven from any rational place within nominal Christianity, wherever the inherently "mortalist" dogmas of Aristotle or the empiricists take over the pulpit.[35]

The practical issue of economic policy here, is this.

Once we acknowledge, that man and woman are made in the image of God, then, we confront ourselves with the obligation to show evidence supporting this specific claim. That evidence must be located within the bounds of a principled difference between the developable functional characteristics of the human individual, and those of all inferior species, perhaps including among the latter, those great apes which Britain's cruel Prince Philip has claimed his wife and children to be. We have indicated, above, the method by which it is shown, that the *monad* of creative reason can be cognized, and its efficiency in the universe demonstrated. It is permitted, I believe, to sing "Hallelujah" at receipt of such good news respecting ***Genesis*** 1:26-30.

What is the quality of people who actually know, rather than merely believe, that they are each made in the image of God? Such people are no "wretches;" they are the stuff of which proud citizens of a true republic are made: citizens who, according to the Preamble of the U.S. Federal ***Constitution***, take care of the matters to be done on the behalf of the dead, the living, and unborn generations, and cause the republic, which they serve, to do so on their behalf, not only for the population of that nation, but the benefit of all humanity. How unlike the nasty Prime Minister Winston Churchill, who hated the Christianity of President Franklin Roosevelt's intent for the post-war period, to right the wrongs of colonialism and rid the planet of the barbarities of "British Eighteenth-Century methods" in economic matters generally. These patriotic citizens of our Amer-

---

of the British monarchy's Privy Council, the Church of England in its capacity as the modern Apollo priesthood.

35. "Mortalism" is the doctrine, that if the human soul does exist, it dies with the body. This was the subject of notable controversies in western Europe during the course of the Sixteenth and Seventeenth Centuries. The seminal argument for mortalism was supplied by the teacher of Venice's Cardinal Gasparo Contarini, Pietro Pomponazzi, the same Pomponazzi who led in reintroducing the Averroes reading of Aristotle into the Venice-dominated sections of the Sixteenth-century Catholic, as well as Protestant clergy. Pomponazzi presented a very capable, and authentically Aristotelean proof, that the individual human soul does not exist, a view which political caution prompted him to modify slightly, at the prompting of his former student Gasparo Contarini. While the Seventeenth-century English tradition of "mortalism" owed much to the heritage of Aristotle, its more immediate origin was the Paolo Sarpi, who, as the leading authority in Venice from 1582 on, did more than any other persons to build up England and the Netherlands as the clones and ultimate successors of the financier-oligarchical power of imperial Venice. Sarpi, a follower of the radically nominalist offshoot of Aristotle's influence, the radical nominalism of William of Ockham, was officially a Servite monk, but actually an atheist, and was the father of the Sixteenth-century English empiricism of Francis Bacon, Thomas Hobbes, and John Locke, and also French Cartesianism. This is the matrix used by Hobbes et al. to outlaw everything, including metaphor, pertaining to the second step of our four-step cycle. If one brings belief in the existence of the "soul" back into empiricism, arbitrarily, the result converges upon the pro-satanic doctrine of the Manicheans and Bogomils (Cathars), which, in fact, was the intellectual model employed by those empiricists, such as Locke, Mandeville, François Quesnay, and Adam Smith, who invented the doctrine of "free trade"/*laissez-faire* on this basis.

ican tradition, are men and women who set forth, like the Good Samaritan on that famous journey, as Cotton Mather rebuked some leading Puritans on this account, *to do good.*

Which would you rather be? The unhappy, mean-spirited creature, mewling pitiably in the offal of his, or her own professed wretchedness, or the proud Christian citizen, as reflected in the inspired Preamble of the U.S. Federal Constitution? Would you worship God because you are a wretch best fit for perdition, or as a veritable angel sent on a mission into mortality, to do good? Are you here, in this mortal life, as punishment for being a wretch, or, are you here because you are needed?

The misled, "low church" fellows speak of "another life." Do you have the abominable conceit, the insolent vanity, to imagine that God Almighty wishes to forsake his entire creation, like some wild-eyed slumlord, for the sake of some "other life" in a better neighborhood? Dare you, slacker, doubt that you were designed and sent to do a job here, in this universe? You think that you can get out of this mortal life, without being held to account for what you should have contributed to mankind and the universe while you were here? You say you are a Christian? What will you give of yourself, for the sake of this nation, of all humanity, if the circumstances point to you, and conscience says, "You are the Good Samaritan of this moment, who must do this on behalf of God and mankind."?

I think that that is now sufficient clinical material cited as background, to allow us to now make the first of the two points, respecting emotion.

The two, contrasted points of view, as exemplifed by the opposing, rational and empiricist, views of individual human nature, implicitly define the opposing quality of passions which define the difference between them. The *erotic* passion which dominates in persons who accept the self-image of "human cattle," is the natural emotional state of the empiricist, for whom "the divine spark of Reason" does not exist. The passion opposite to *eros*, is *agapē*, to which the Apostle Paul refers, in the celebrated ***I Corinthians*** 13; the domination of the person's emotional life by the passion called *agapē*, is the naturally healthy state of emotion of the citizen of the republic.

In general, the level of culture in the United States today has fallen so low, so precipitously, during the recent thirty-odd years, that the only likely spoken referent for *agapē* which would be easily acknowledged by even a large minority of the population, would be

"tears of joy." Otherwise, the much smaller ration of the population which would be more likely to recognize a state of being corresponding to Plato's or the Apostle Paul's use of *agapē*, would be among Classical performing artists in the same tradition as the celebrated conductor Wilhelm Furtwängler, or scientists whose musical interest converges upon the standard of insight referenced by Furtwängler's celebrated notion of "performing between the notes."[36]

On this account, respecting *ideas*, such as those associated with *agapē*, educated scientists and artists today, are, with rare exceptions, qualitatively inferior to performers of corresponding relative standing from earlier generations. In music, for example, my relevant best sources emphasize, the best young performers have relatively outstanding physical performance skills, but are usually an interpretative disaster. They have learned to play the notes, with great skill; would they had better traded some of that skill for better ability to perform the music. What I hear from performances, is in accord with that report.

A reference to the four-step outline serves us again, on this specific account. That four-step approach is rep-

---

36. The phrase "behind the notes" is an alternative one. This means, as he elaborated his argument, that the performer must relive the composer's process of compositional development. The method of Classical motivic thorough-composition, already implied in such locations as J.S. Bach's *A Musical Offering* and *The Art of the Fugue*, is based upon a sequence of inversions and other ontological paradoxes arising within a well-tempered polyphonic domain. Replication of the notes of the composition must be the adumbration of the *idea* of *ideas*: the ideas which are defined by metaphorical resolutions of an ontologically paradoxical ordering of ontological paradoxes. The shaping of the intervals, both within the voice, and among the voices, and the inversions of those intervals, must be brought into a coherent order, for achieving that singleness of effect, of the performed composition as a whole, which evokes from within the musical hearer an appropriate sense of the subsuming idea of the composer's act of composing the work as an integrated whole. The goal of great Classical work's artistic performance, is that the performer must command the audience's concentration at the moment the first tone is sounded, and the individual member of that audience must not be aware of the seat in which he, or she is seated, until after the resonance of the last tone has gone into the past. As the surviving performance record attests, Furtwängler was a master of precisely this quality of performance, to the degree of perfecting the enunciation of the attack upon the first tone by the orchestra, this to the purpose of making the idea of the completed performance that of the composer's intent. His handling of the Franz Schubert "Great" C-Major Symphony is exemplary of the way in which Furtwängler was unexcelled and rarely matched on this account. The point to be stressed here, is that this example references precisely the approach required for dealing with any valid fundamental discovery of principle in physical science, or in any branch of Classical art.

resentative of Classical-humanist education. In such education, typified best by Wilhelm von Humboldt's reform of education in Germany, the student, instead of "learning the answer," is required to relive the experience of the original discoverer, or, as near an approximation of the original discoverer's experience as possible. In other words, the student must relive that as the four-step outline implies. In that case, the successful student repeatedly experiences the specific quality of concentrated emotion which is *agapē*.

This experience of *agapē*, in that way, has two aspects. In the case of reliving scientific discoveries of valid physical principle, it is known as the specific quality of passion one experiences within oneself, whenever concentration is motivated in the way which leads to the resolving discovery of principle. This is the exact same quality of emotion experienced in the act of insight into analogous resolutions embedded in a Classical musical composition, or, in first recognizing the resolution of the metaphor of a Classical tragedy, or poem, or the same kind of mental act in the study of the method of metaphor underlying great paintings by Leonardo da Vinci and Raphael Sanzio.

In the first class of cases, physical science, the emotion is recognized. In the second, Classical art and related matters of *Geisteswissenschaft*, *agapē* is summoned by the compositional principle of metaphor, that *agapē* itself might educate the larger scope of emotional associations of the person's mind. Thus, Friedrich Schiller's follower, Wilhelm von Humboldt, specified, that the primary function of the Classical humanist form of combined scientific and artistic secondary education, was to develop the moral character of the student: not by indoctrination in do's and don't's, mistakenly called "character-building" by some misguided people, but by cultivating the pervasiveness of the idea of *agapē* within oneself, as the Apostle Paul demands in *I Corinthians* 13. From this latter true morality springs.

The trouble today is, that the virtual elimination of pedagogical competence unique to Classical-humanist methods (our four-step method) from the pre-science and science curricula, and also artistic habits of the population, has produced a population which has concentrated so much on learning to pass the examination, that it has little power of concentration remaining for actual thinking. In this way, it has lost touch with the importance of actually knowing what it is that they are learning. Indeed, the moral debasement of educational policy in the U.S.A. today, is typified by the eradication of the principle of truthfulness: one is judged on how well one appears to have learned the approved material, without any consideration of whether the opinions expressed by the material are truthful, or not.

As a result, the essential distinction of the present "under-55" generations, relative to that of the World War II veterans' generation, is that the newer generations have zero to little capacity for actual happiness in life; their capacity for happiness has shrunk in approximately the same degree their appetite—one might say, their desperation—for momentary pleasure has skyrocketted.

Real happiness lies in the joy of being human, of being a creature made in the image of God. We touch happiness in the experience of those same qualities which are summoned by reliving discovery of scientific principle, by Classical artistic experience, and by any form of constructive problem-solving which draws upon what is supplied by the mental powers expressed in step two of the four-step process.

This pursuit of happiness is individual, but also intrinsically social. To enjoy a discovery, is to anticipate sharing it, or, at least, some benefit of it, with others. That social result is the element of "pursuit" in the experience of happiness. This is the proper goal of individual life: a happiness which transcends that succession of activities associated with it. Today, one job is to be accomplished; next, another. The happiness lies not in any job as such, but in the process of moving from one to the next, and, on to the next, beyond that. One rejoices if one has the means and opportunity to live such a useful life.

That is a life of happiness, a right with which the Declaration of Independence, and also the Preamble of our Federal Constitution endow each person by law, such as happiness in the fulfillment of uncompleted good work bequeathed to us by a deceased predecessor. Thus, in science, we *name* the discoverers whose work we bring happily to a greater degree of fulfillment. We name the heroes from the past, whose labor, and, sometimes, painful suffering, is justified by our happily realizing the fruitfulness of what they had left uncompleted. We are filled with joy at the thought that some yet unborn persons will derive happiness, long after we are dead, flowing from some good work to which we are devoting our efforts today.

Such is the emotion called *agapē*. The joyful passion which is typified by the happy condition of commitment to truth and justice. But, there is something more to this than is suggested by the popular sense of the meaning of the term "emotion."

Popular opinion regards all emotion as simply, quantifiably extended impulses. That presumption is in fundamental error. Although unregulated (e.g., "ignorant") erotic impulses tend to be crudely linear in the sense imputed by popular opinion, *agapē* is never linear; it has a recognizable sense of curvature in the Kepler-Leibniz-Gauss-Riemann sense. The case of the great musical works of Classical motivic thorough-composition, as from Mozart during the early 1780s, through the last compositions of Brahms, most conveniently demonstrates this correlation between agapic emotion and curvature. *Agapē* is an impulse of action; it acts as a principle of action, an action which has a definable "curvature" in a higher sense of that term.

This bears upon the promised second, intellectual, aspect of the matter.

The representation of this fact is made feasible by the notion of an ordered succession of Riemannian manifolds. *This curvature is of the type we have referenced as anti-entropic.* We are back to Plato, and, this time, to the notion of *higher hypothesis*, to the domain which Leibniz sometimes named "*Analysis Situs.*" This is the domain implicit in Plato's **Parmenides**. It is a domain of what may appear, at first acquaintance, as a realm of eerie sophistication; but, that uneasiness should be put down largely to the fact that, for most readers, the concepts involved are new.

Let us follow the simplest version of Riemann's representation. This, fortunately, will suffice to show what must be said here. If there were no falsehoods in taught doctrines of mathematical physics, then there would be no manifolds which are categorically false, but rather inadequately developed. Thus, in that case, the fault in a manifold of n dimensions would lie essentially in the fact, that a valid manifold of $n+1$ dimensions were better. In such a conjecturable case, the simplest notion of an ordered Riemannian series would be of the form *…n, $n+1$, $n+2$,….*.

However, as we have already considered this, we can not define the characteristics of a manifold simply in terms of its valid dimensions. In each case, we must also consider the experimental determination of its curvature. A purely formal mathematical physics, such as might be extrapolated by some marvellous computer, should be regarded as a contradiction in terms. This brings us directly to the **Parmenides** syndrome: *what (one) common factor underlies the generation of an or-*

derable series of such manifolds?

That "factor"—that "One" of the **Parmenides**—is those cognitive powers of the individual human mind, the which are expressed in step two of the four-step process. Thus, the characteristic change in curvature, in proceeding from manifold n to successive manifolds $n+1$ and $n+2$, and so on, is the curvature expressing the action of that cognitive function. *The general character of that cognitive action is, therefore, shown to be, experimentally, anti-entropic.*

Such an ordering principle, which subsumes an ordered array of manifolds (hypotheses), is Plato's "higher hypothesis." This higher hypothesis has a relationship to the array of individual hypotheses which it underlies, which, at first impression, resembles the relationship of any simple hypothesis to a corresponding theorem-lattice. This notion of "higher hypothesis" defines Leibniz's domain of *Analysis Situs*. This function distinguishes the efficient existence of the principle of individual cognition as an agapic *monad*, whose curvature, however variable, is functionally distinct.[37]

This monad-activity is thus defined as the principle of change which characterizes the efficient interaction between mankind and the universe as a whole. This interaction, in turn, is defined by the cognitive action of the individual's mind upon this whole interaction with mankind's functional relationship to the universe. The crucial questions thus posed, pertain to the matter of the marvellous agreement between the principle of cognition, as governing mankind's anti-entropic solutions for paradoxes, and the principle of self-generation underlying the existence of the universe as a whole. That connection celebrates man and woman made in the image of the Creator.

The general outline of this proposition was already comprehended by Plato, from whom types such as Riemann and I learned, if somewhat indirectly (e.g., from Leibniz), the conceptions which prompted our approaches to converge upon a common solution.

We can now summarize the implications of this specific, crucial aspect of the whole matter before us, with no need for further elaboration than that, of that particular point here. *It is this anti-entropic curvature of agapic mental action, expressed by experimentally successful*

---

37. Hence: "hypothesizing the higher hypothesis." Hence, the correspondence between "hypothesizing the higher hypothesis" and the Becoming. Hence, that which underlies, and rules the timeless eternity in which the Becoming dwells, the Good.

cognition of the type illustrated by the four-step model, which is the source of the anti-entropic curvature of successful physical economy.

This is expressed in bold terms by the outgrowth of the United States' pioneering development of a full-blown Carnot type of machine-tool-design-driven economy, during 1861-1876, and most boldly by the impact of science-driver "crash programs" as the more concentrated form of machine-tool-design-driven economies.

Thus, this relationship between the curvature in the infinitesimal interval of action, cognition, and the curvature of the process in the large, is situated within Leibniz's domain of *Analysis Situs.*

Time To Conclude for the Present

The crucial significance of these notions of hypothesis, is that they lead us effectively to the means by which we are able to extricate the notion of "time" from the undesirable company of that compulsive sophistry of the mathematics classroom, "self-evident truth." In connection with relevant issues of economics, there are two mutually-dependent notions of "time" to be considered. First, the bare notion of time as an experimentally-based principle. Second, the notion of apparent "time-reversal," which inheres not only in the notion of higher hypothesis, but which is, empirically, the most significant of the subsumed features, as complement to agapic curvature, of human cognitive behavior itself.[38]

In first approximation. Given a theorem-set, underlain by its hypothesis. Consider Euclidean geometry as such a theorem-lattice. Two subsumed notions confront us.

First, as Euclid's geometry illustrates the notion, although each and all theorems have a demonstrably immediate relationship to the conditions imposed by the underlying hypothesis of the theorem-set, the generation (construction) of the theorems is subject to notions of sequential ordering. These sequences are defined by the need to have constructed, or otherwise generated, the preconditions for stating the problem whose solution determines the generation of the new theorem. These sequences are also defined, by actions which must be taken to bring the entire theorem-lattice from the state prior to the generation of the new theorem, into the new state after the addition of the new theorem.

"Is that experience with Euclidean and later geometries, borne out in the domain of physics and the composition and performance of Classical art?" The characteristic of human behavior is ordering, hence action, as defined by sequences.

Second, the fact that the theorem-lattice has some such notion of sequence associated with its ordering, underscores the fact of the hypothesis's existing simultaneously in all times occupied by the generation of any and all theorems of the corresponding lattice.

For purposes of pedagogy, we could illustrate the latter point's relevance, by stating, that if the duration of the theorem-set's development could be virtually without limit, then the underlying hypothesis would be associated with a notion of virtual simultaneity of virtual near-eternity.[39] This notion, in turn, leads to the conjecturable notion of possibly efficient, real forms of time-reversal.

In second approximation. Consider an hypothesis-lattice, such as an orderable succession of Riemannian manifolds. What are the characteristic features of human behavior, especially physical-economic behavior, as viewed from this vantage-point, in respect to time?

In this case, we have an anti-entropic ordering (curvature) of the hypothesis-lattice as such, and, also, an anti-entropic curvature of the process subject to this lattice's development. Again, the condition of ordered hypothesizing of the higher hypothesis, exists in simultaneity with all possible hypotheses and their ordered development. Again, hypothesizing the higher hypothesis, is associated with its simultaneity in virtual eternity. Again, but this time more forcibly, we are confronted by the notion of a functionally efficient role of time-reversal.

This was the last of the mathematical-physical considerations referenced in the Bad Godesberg presentation. It returns now, as the concluding point to be clarified here.

As I have elaborated the formal argument for this earlier,[40] the fact that the ordering of a succession of Riemannian manifolds is subsumed (underlain) by the

---

38. Cf. Lyndon H. LaRouche, Jr., "The Essential Role of 'Time Reversal' in Mathematical Economics," ***Executive Intelligence Review***, Oct. 11, 1996.

39. The notion of "simultaneity of eternity," is an implication of Plato's Socratic dialectic, which, among other considerations, occupies a significant niche within Christian theology.

40. "The Essential Role of 'Time-Reversal' in Mathematical Economics," op. cit.

higher hypothesis embedded in step two, locates that higher hypothesis in the "simultaneity of eternity." In other words, (through hypothesizing it) the higher hypothesis efficiently underlies future, past, and present, with approximately equal efficiency, simultaneously.

"Exotic"? Only to those who are unfamiliar with the main lines of history of European thought since Plato.

"Not essential"? On the contrary, the practical implications of this are the central issue of all physical science, all Classical art, and all statecraft and related matters of economy.

"Unfamiliar"? Precisely; but, like a society's ignorance of medicine, unfamiliarity is no benefit to those populists who prefer to rely upon "traditional culture's" less expensive home remedies.

This notion of higher hypothesis is reflected in the first principle of scientific knowledge: that the tragedian Aeschylos must allow Prometheus' foreknowledge of the future to govern his behavior in the present.[41] This conception escapes the realm of ambiguity when we have shifted the point of reference from choices of theorems of simple hypothesis, to policies rooted in discoveries of principle. That is, when we have apprehended the future state of a process through the quality of cognitive action represented by a discovery of principle, a valid solution to a Classical form of artistic metaphor.

The practical implication of this for economic policy-making, is most readily underscored by the fact, that a policy of free trade has never been successful for any economy subjected to it for a medium- to long-term period. Every successful period of growth in modern national economies, has occurred under what are termed "dirigist" policies of governments, combined with the kinds of "protectionist" measures of regulating trade and foreign exchange associated with economists and statesmen such as U.S. Treasury Secretary Alexander Hamilton, Mathew Carey, Henry Clay, John Quincy Adams, and Henry C. Carey.

By its very nature, productive investment is action taken in the present to bring about a near approximation of a projected future condition. *Wisdom, cognition, is remembering the present, and also the past, in one's actions to bring about a desired future condition. "Wisdom" is living in "the simultaneity of eternity."* The crucial demonstration, which unquestionably sepa-

rates men from beasts on this account, involves those cases in which the present intention of a future consequence is premised upon the use of a discovered principle, such as a physical principle. This places the actions, linking future to present, within the domain of our step two, the domain of higher hypothesis.

Before the introduction of Paolo Sarpi's empiricism, and empiricism's mechanistic notion of the term "cause," modern European experimental science, such as that of Leonardo da Vinci, Johannes Kepler, and William Gilbert, located the ordering of relations between apparent causes and their consequential effects under the rubric of Reason, as Leibniz did. Leibniz refined this notion of Reason to meet the requirements of experimental physics, with his term "sufficient and necessary reason." Gauss's unique success in forecasting the orbit of Ceres, is a stunning affirmation of the notion of Reason as it appears in the work of Kepler and Leibniz. In mathematical physics, this idea of Reason is represented mathematically by the notion of physical-space-time curvature in the infinitesimally small.

To wit:

Why should the future orbital position of a planet, for example, be manifest in the curvature of a very small interval of its present trajectory? This implies, that the existence of the orbit precedes the planet's inclination to follow that pathway.

The contrary, the empiricist-materialist idea, that this is the result of some repetitive kinematic (e.g., "free trade") "pushme-pullme" arrangement, was the issue of method underscored by Gauss's success in the Ceres matter. Although Newton's general formulation for gravitation was derived, algebraically, from Kepler's formulation for gravitation, algebraic consistency did not prevent Newton's derivation from falling into the "three-body problem" fallacy, which did not exist for Kepler's representation.

Examining the entirety of Kepler's design retrospectively, from the standpoint of Leibniz, Gauss, and Riemann, the origin of Newton's failure is clear immediately. Throughout the work represented by the ***Mysterium Cosmographicum***, the two editions of the ***New Astronomy***, and the ***World Harmony***, and also the summary address to the problem in Kepler's "Snowflake" paper, there should be nothing mysterious left respecting the origin of this difference.

Kepler's notion of *Reason* as the agency determining the harmonically ordered sequence of available

---

41. Aeschylos, ***Prometheus Bound***.

What Really Happened in China?   47

solar orbits, locates Reason as it is expressed by Plato's notion of higher hypothesis, and as Leibniz chose his term "*Analysis Situs*" to identify an aspect of this.

The result of this approach, by Kepler, Leibniz, Gauss, Riemann, et al., is to abandon the mechanistic, kinematic, algebraic view of physical action as located within a Cartesian-like notion of space and time, and to treat available lawful trajectories as reflections of a principled, specific form of higher hypothesis, underlying the modular ordering of successive (e.g., Riemannian) hypotheses: i.e., *Analysis Situs.*

That said, the reader is to be reminded, that our primary standpoint in this report, is that of an ordering of successive Riemannian hypotheses, as ordered by an higher hypothesis, of implicitly anti-entropic curvature, the which is coincident with a corresponding quality of development of the cognitive capability expressed by step two of the four-step process. In other words, that all effective economic policy of practice must reflect the way in which the human mind applies to the future state of an economy to determine the present.

The effect of this consideration upon the proper design of economic policy, is properly filed under the classification "Freedom and Necessity." "Freedom" is that which expresses the cognitive potentials of step two. "Necessity" is the curvature which the realization of "Freedom" imposes upon the results; "Necessity" is, therefore, the future state of a society applied to determine the choice of action made in the present.

In the economic domain so defined, science must smile an agapic smile, at the genius with which the Leibniz-inspired American System of political-economy[42]—of Franklin, Hamilton, the Careys, and List—

has apportioned the separate but interdependent economic functions of private initiative and the state. The greatest rate of individual creative innovation, is desired in the processes of production and design of product, the private sector. The success of this private enterprise depends upon the certainty that the basic economic infrastructure, including not only transportation, power, water management, but also education, promotion of scientific progress, national defense, security in public health, regulation and defense of a system of money and credit, and regulation of foreign trade, is developed, by state guarantees, for the needs of all the territory, and all the people.

Both the public and private departments of economy use Reason, to impose the necessary future upon the presently preferred choices of action for change. The division between private and public, assorts the responsibility for progress in such a fashion, as to give the relatively greatest latitude for the individual creative powers in the private sector, and the responsibility for serving the interest of all the people, and all the territory, to the public sector. If some arrangement could be more prudent, history has yet to discover it.

Thus, Reason produces science, and science then produces Necessity.

If we remove from the history of the modern nation-state and national economy, all of those corruptions which are reflections of the backward impulses of so-called "traditional cultures," and the malicious effects of oligarchical insolence, the modern state and modern national state would show themselves more clearly to have been, by a far length, the greatest boon to mankind, the greatest contribution to the increase of individual freedom, which statecraft has yet to produce. The fault lies not with the nation-state, or with national-economy; the fault lies with our tolerating the feudal relics of financier oligarchy much too long. The fault with the toleration of the oligarchical succubus, is not merely that it has robbed nations' purses, but, as we have noted respecting the oligarchical abuse of religion, the worst thing it has done, is to rob most of our people of their sanity.

If this lesson of science and history were to become generally understood, at least among statesmen, then that temporary suffering we can not avoid during this present crisis were a relatively small price to pay for the opportunity to free humanity, for once and forever, from the succubus of financier oligarchy.

---

42. The struggle to determine the future of the English-speaking colonies in North America, became, from the early Eighteenth Century on, a conflict between the opposing political and economic philosophies of empiricist John Locke and Christian Gottfried Leibniz. The former viewpoint came to identify, to the present day, the frequently treasonous "American Tory" faction of the New England opium-trafficker, Manhattan banker, and southern slave-holder components of the oligarchical faction. The latter, the patriot's tradition of Franklin, Washington, Hamilton, Henry Clay, the Careys, John Quincy Adams, Abraham Lincoln, and so on. For the "American Tory" generally, as for the Constitution of the short-lived British puppet-state, the Confederate States of America (CSA), the watchword was Locke's "Life, Liberty, and Property." For the patriot, the watchword of the U.S. Declaration of Independence and "welfare clause" of the U.S. Constitution's Preamble, was Leibniz's devastating rebuttal of Hobbes and Locke, "Life, Liberty, and the Pursuit of Happiness."